THE

Buddhist Path
to Simplicity

THE
Buddhist Path
to Simplicity

Spiritual Practice For Everyday Life

CHRISTINA FELDMAN

Thorsons
An Imprint of HarperCollins*Publishers*
77–85 Fulham Palace Road
Hammersmith, London w6 8jb

The website address is: www.thorsonselement.com

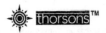

and *Thorsons* are trademarks of
HarperCollins*Publishers* Limited.

First published 2001
This edition 2004

A catalogue record for this book
is available from the British Library

ISBN 13: 978-0-007-32361-6

Printed and bound in Great Britain by
Creative Print and Design (Wales), Ebbw Vale

Contents

Foreword

IN our modern consumer society, many people long for greater simplicity and freedom. In a world of strife and conflict, many long for forgiveness and compassion.

You hold in your hands a reminder that this is truly possible. Christina Feldman's gracious invitation to freedom is like the flower held in the hand of the Buddha. She reminds us that the beauty we seek is at hand ... if only we can remove the dust from our eyes and step out of the palace of illusion.

To do so asks of us a few simple, sacred tasks. To look at the sorrows of the world with eyes of compassion for ourselves and others. To learn the art of trust and letting go. To discover the beauty of the middle way. To remember that like the Buddha, we can rest in a peaceful heart, halfway between heaven and earth, without judging, grasping, or fearing.

From this sacred middle way, we see that we are not separate from all that lives. From this awakened presence, natural care and integrity are born. In any moment this flower of awakening and simplicity beckons to us. May you listen to these words with care and find their truth in your own heart.

JACK KORNFIELD
Spirit Rock Meditation Center
Woodacre, California
2001

introduction

We accept the graceful falling

Of mountain cherry blossoms,

But it is much harder for us

To fall away from our own

Attachment to the world

ZEN

WE frequently long for a simpler life, to find those moments when we can sit beneath a tree and listen for one wholehearted moment. We yearn to find the space to attend to our own inner rhythms and messages, the space to reflect upon the direction of our lives and to be touched by the subtle changes of each passing moment. We long to find the space to listen to another person and to our own hearts with total attention. Intuitively, we know these spaces teach us about what is significant, about how to find our path in this world, what nurtures us and how to be touched by the world around us.

Moments of stillness and genuine simplicity offer us glimpses of what it means to live in a sacred and free way. We know we do not need yet more sounds, thoughts, experiences, possessions, or attainments. We have had so many and they fail to quench our thirst for freedom and stillness. They do not make us happier, more free or compassionate. Instead, we discover that the clutter of our lives and minds entangles us in an escalating cycle of haste, alienation, and exhaustion.

In our hearts we know that genuine freedom is much deeper than a permission to have more, accumulate more, or become more. Freedom is the ability to live in such a way that there is no sense of imprisonment. To be free in our lives is to live authentically, embodying creativity, wisdom, and compassion in all dimensions of our lives. Freedom implies a genuine understanding of the source of happiness, the end of despair and conflict. Freedom and simplicity are close companions; simplicity teaches us the ways to release the layers of complexity and confusion that blind us. In their falling away we discover the innate vastness of freedom within us.

We are the most materially affluent of all generations. In pursuit of the "good" life, we have the possibility of more possessions, attainments, and choices than ever before. We are also a generation of great despair, alienation, and unhappiness. We tend to be hoarders, amassing, accumulating, and gathering endless stockpiles of "stuff," inwardly and outwardly, which itself becomes a source of anxiety and tension. The clutter we accumulate, the endless possessions that no longer serve us, the distractions that fill our days, the incomplete conversations and relationships, the long list of things we "meant" to do, take over our lives, our homes, and our hearts.

There is a story of a wise king who, nearing the end of his life, invited his most devoted subjects to his palace so he could choose an heir. Before the meetings began they were offered fine clothes to dress in, dined on the best of foods, and were entertained by the finest performers. Several hours later, the king asked his attendant to invite his subjects before him so he could question them as to how they would rule the land. Red-faced, the attendant confessed that all the people had gone home. Lost in the pleasures and distractions of the evening they had quite forgotten why they were there.

A path of conscious simplicity teaches us how to recover ourselves and our lives. A new profession of lifestyle advisors has emerged to aid those who find themselves drowning in the clutter and complexity of their lives and hearts. These professionals remind us that having is not the same as happiness and that simplicity may bring the inner space from which authenticity and creativity emerge. Clearly, the meaning of our lives cannot be defined by the accumulation of things and achievements. The meaning of our lives is defined by the quality of our presence in this world and in each moment.

We need to learn how to be our own inner lifestyle consultant. What do we lean upon for security, identity, and reassurance? What are the sources of confusion and unhappiness in our lives? Does the source of happiness lie in the accolades, objects, and attainments we gather or do the roots of genuine happiness lie in our own heart? There are times when it is wise to step back from our preoccupations and listen more deeply to the rhythms and quality of our hearts and minds. In these moments the cultivation of stillness is a great gift of kindness we offer to ourselves. We discover the wisdom of ceasing to externalize the source of happiness, reclaiming instead our own capacity to nurture inner well-being and wholeness. In learning to let go of the complexity and busyness in our lives, we are also learning to let go of confusion and agitation.

We have the capacity to shape our lives, and the choices we make directly impact on the quality and well-being of the world; a world that is in dire need of people committed to compassion, integrity, and freedom. Simplicity in our lives expresses respect and care for our world; simplicity in our hearts expresses respect and compassion for ourselves and all living beings.

The search for simplicity is a sacred quest that embraces the many dimensions of our lives and hearts. In seeking simplicity we are not asked to abandon our lives but to reflect on the many strategies, objects, and pursuits that preoccupy us. Do they serve us well? Do they make us more happy or free? What can we let go of, re-examine, complete? It is not enough to unclutter our outer lives and leave intact the restlessness, anxiety, and insecurity at the heart of our confusion. Instead, we are asked to reflect upon our inner life—where can we be more mindful, how can we learn to be wholeheartedly attentive, what we need to let go of, what is the source of genuine happiness and freedom.

Our speech, ethics, livelihoods, the efforts we make in our

lives, our thoughts, feelings, attitudes, and beliefs—this is our world that asks for wise attention and understanding. Throughout the following chapters, the path of simplicity in the teachings of the Buddha is explored. It is a path of wisdom that teaches us to be a Buddha in our own lives. It is a path of awakening and compassion. The falling away of our layers of confusion and complexity will reveal to us the possibility of a life of freedom and compassion.

A disciple once asked the Buddha to explain the depth and profundity of his teaching. After sitting in silence for a few moments, he simply held up a flower and smiled. We may think of the path to peace and freedom as long, complex, and arduous. Instead, we can simply turn our attention to this moment, this life, and let it speak to us of wonder, mystery, harmony, and peace. There is no better moment in which to awaken and discover everything our heart longs for, than the moment we are in.

simplicity

The birds have vanished into the sky,

And now the last cloud fades away.

We sit together, the mountain and I,

until only the mountain remains.

LI PO

LIVING in Asia as a young woman, my entire life could fit into a single backpack and be moved within minutes. The momentous challenges of the day involved choosing between three varieties of lentils to cook, selecting which of four outfits to wear, and deciding when to meditate. Today, it would take more than one removal van to transport my life; endless planning and words such as "priorities," "commitments," and "meetings" have become a regular part of my vocabulary.

We are the first generation of spiritual aspirants to attempt to find a life of awakening and freedom while living in the world rather than within the cloistered walls of a monastery. There are few sure voices or blueprints to guide us. We are learning the lessons of engaged renunciation—treasuring simplicity within a life of consciously loving, working, and creating. The dilemma each one of us faces is how to meet our heart's longing for calm simplicity amid a complex life. It is a journey that may involve a change in our lives. It will surely involve a change of heart. It is a journey that asks for honesty, commitment, wisdom, and a willingness to learn.

Spiritual traditions throughout history remind us that we can live with joyous simplicity; a life where our mind is our friend, our hearts are loving; where we are at home in our body and at peace with each changing moment of life. Simplicity is the mother of creativity and immediacy, intimacy and understanding, compassion and depth. The key to profound happiness and freedom lies in our capacity to discover simplicity in each moment.

Idealizing simplicity, we dream of mountain caves far removed from life's demands and challenges. We envy the hermits and monks who appear unflustered by timetables, commitments, and responsibilities. Yet any monastic would tell us that renouncing the material world has its hardships, but letting go of the agitation and complexity of the mind is much, much harder. A newly-ordained monk confided that beneath the serene appearance he presented in his first years, much of his inner life had been dedicated to designing his home of the future, replaying conversations of the past, and engaging in endless arguments with the discipline he outwardly bowed to.

Simplicity may be projected into the future where we believe we will reclaim our time and our lives from the obligations or circumstances that now define them—our families, work, and economic demands. Dreams of enlightened retirement appear in those moments when we feel overwhelmed by the complexity of our lives. We may even believe that the path to simplicity lies solely in solving the outer predicaments and challenges. It is easy to forget that the tyranny of complexity in our lives does not lie as much in our life circumstances, timetables, and obligations, but in our relationships to them and the paths of living we choose and embody.

The shape of our world and our experience of it is molded in our hearts and minds. The commuter on the train may be taking that moment to be still, to cultivate calmness and sensitivity. The hermit in the cave may spend countless moments daydreaming of a better life or replaying some old, familiar song of resentment. Outer change carries no guarantee of inner change; in the quest for simplicity we are invited to examine the rhythm and quality of our own life. It is authentic inner transformation, born of investigation and understanding, that translates our dreams of simplicity and freedom into reality.

The world that invites profound transformation is the one we carry within us. The only moment that offers the possibility of transformation and simplicity is this moment. Calm simplicity is not born of rejecting this moment or this world, but of our own willingness to probe the causes of agitation and complexity. We do not need to look further than this moment, this world, to find the simplicity we hunger for. Simplicity and stillness are not born of transcending our life but of a radical change in our hearts and minds. The endless strategies we engage in to ease the tension and unrest in our hearts are like rearranging the furniture in an overcrowded room. Every great meditative path encourages us to turn directly towards all that preoccupies and burdens us. Learning to cultivate inner calmness, to care wholeheartedly for the moment we are in, to learn to release anxiety and agitation; these are lessons we can only learn while living our lives.

The Source of Happiness and Unhappiness

The Buddha said so simply and clearly that the source of happiness and unhappiness lies nowhere else but in our minds and hearts. We can make endless journeys to find happiness, and engage in countless strategies to rid ourselves of unhappiness, but—the key traveler on all the journeys and the central player in all the strategies is ourselves, and it is to ourselves we always return. There is a wonderful Zen saying, "The only Truth you find on top of the mountain is the truth you brought with you." We discover happiness through making peace with ourselves and the circumstances of our lives, not through trying to escape from them, nor through living in fantasies about the future. Our lives will continue to present us with unexpected challenges and opportunities. Our bodies will age and become fragile, our teenagers will rebel, our colleagues may frustrate us, financial demands will continue to appear. We will meet with allies and adversaries. We will be asked to find room in our hearts for the needs of others, to embrace our own demons, and to respond to the changing circumstances of each moment. We make peace with our lives through learning to connect with the simple truths of each moment. As the graffiti on the bridge tells us, "We are not in a traffic jam. We are the traffic jam."

We do not have to travel far to discover simplicity. Each encounter, event, and moment is a mirror that reflects our reactions, fears, longings, and stories. When we encounter another person, in that moment we also meet ourselves in our thoughts, feelings, and responses. Exploring and touching our own heart and mind, we become intimate with all hearts and minds. Fear and anger, greed and jealousy, loving kindness and generosity, compassion and forgiveness are not personal possessions, but universal, human feelings. Understanding how our world is created on a moment-to-moment level, we understand all worlds.

The present moment we are in offers everything we need to discover the deepest serenity and most profound simplicity. There is not a better moment, a more perfect moment for us to awaken and uncover the immediacy and well-being we long for. Tolstoy once said, "If you want to be happy; be." Yearning for simplicity we are guided to turn our attention to those events, circumstances, and inner experiences that appear most entangled. The places where we feel the most lost and confused are the places we are asked to shine the light of clear and kind attention.

The Buddha said, "I teach only one thing—there is suffering and there is an end of suffering." All Buddhist traditions and practices rest upon this one simple statement. We all live in the same world experiencing sounds, sights, tastes, smells, feelings, and thoughts. We share the same story of birth, aging, sickness, and death. We all have the capacity for delight and distress, great compassion and great struggle. In the universal story none of us will remain untouched by loss, sadness, and pain, and we will all be touched by moments of simple joy and gladness—we will all laugh and we will all weep. It is a story of change and unpredictability, and it will not always be under our control. This is the story of life.

Simplicity will not be found in trying to mold life to comply with our desires and expectations. The events and circumstances of our world feel no obligation to conform to our expectations. Again and again we learn that the gap between what is and what "should be" is an ocean of distress, disappointment, and frustration. These feelings are not intrinsic to living but derive from our unwillingness to turn our hearts and minds to the realities of each moment. To have the wisdom to acknowledge the bare truths of the moment—"this is grief," "this is fear," "this is frustration"—enables us to lay down the burden of our stories and "shoulds," and follow the road to peace. Simplicity is born of a depth of understanding that enables us to harmonize our inner world with the changes and unpredictability of life.

Personal Story, Life Story

Our personal story is rooted within the universal story, but we each bring to it different ways of experiencing and holding it. To each moment we bring our past memories, hopes, fears, and preferences, and the world reflects back to us the state of our minds. A traveler came to the gates of a new city and asked the gatekeeper, "What kind of people live here?" The gatekeeper answered with a question of his own, "What kind of people lived in the city you just came from?" The traveler replied, "They were mostly a cantankerous lot, greedy and self-centered." The gatekeeper answered, "I expect you will find the people here just the same." Soon after, another traveler met the gatekeeper and asked the same question. Again the gatekeeper asked, "How did you find the residents of the city you visited last?" The traveler answered enthusiastically, "They were warm and hospitable; truly a fine group of people." The gatekeeper responded, "I expect you will find these folk just the same."

Love and loss, frustration and contentment, intimacy and separation, praise and blame, beginnings and endings—this is the story of life. For each person who meets life with joy and ease, there is another who lives with fear and conflict. The story of life offers us possibilities of entanglement and intensity, or simplicity and ease. To discover the peace of simplicity we are asked to see through the layers of misunderstanding and confusion that camouflage the serenity that is possible for us. The Buddha said, "We carry in our eyes the dust of entanglement." Entanglement comes with our historical resentments, images, and fears that distort our present. Again and again we find ourselves superimposing our experiences and stories from the past upon the present. Losing ourselves in the stories, we deny to ourselves the capacity to see fully the person in front of us, the moment we are experiencing, or ourselves.

Someone offends us. The next day we encounter them again. No sooner do we set eyes upon them than we find ourselves replaying our resentment, the story of yesterday, at the forefront of our mind. Can we see that person without the veils of the story? Can we see them as someone who may not even know that they have hurt us or as someone caught up in the same agitation we ourselves have experienced? Do we find ourselves already avoiding, rejecting, or judging? Can we learn to breathe out, to let go of the story, and find the generosity to be wholeheartedly present with that person?

Disentanglement comes with the calm patience and attention that illuminates those places and moments where we founder, learning to let go and establish ourselves in the simple truths of each moment. Being present does not imply that we erase our past and the impact it has had upon us. Being present invites us to allow the memories and the stories rooted in the past to be just whispers in our minds that we no longer solidify with unwise attention. We free ourselves to turn a whole-hearted attention to this moment.

Calm simplicity and peace are not only reserved for those with fortunate lives, bulging spiritual portfolios, or for the karmically blessed. Serenity, compassion, and stillness are not accidents but consciously cultivated paths. They are possible for each of us, born of wisdom, dedication, and the willingness to clear the dust of entanglement. It is there for all, born of wisdom, dedication, and the willingness to see clearly.

If a group of people were taken to the foot of a mountain, each person intending to climb to the top, every individual would approach the ascent guided by their own personal story and by their inner sense of possibility or limitation. There would be the person who takes one look at the trail and retires in despair without even taking a single step. There would be the person equipped for every eventuality with parachute, pitons, rations, and a hot water bottle. There would be the person who throws away the map and attacks the hardest route, driven by the ambition to be first to the top. There would be the climber who manages to ascend halfway before getting lost in the pleasant views, quite forgetting the rest of the journey. There would be the climber who has spent countless hours rehearsing and planning each step of the journey. There might also be that rare person who sees how far there is to go, but remains unhurried, carefully placing each foot on the ground; who delights in the views and the sounds but never gets lost; whose journey is completed in every step.

This last is the path of simplicity—always available to us in each sight, step, event, and moment. It is a path of peace and completeness. The habits of our lives become solid and familiar with time through endless repetition. We see them in our relationships, work, speech, and choices. We learn where these habits lead to agitation, complexity, and entanglement. We also discover that just because these habits have a long history, this does not imply that they have a long future. The willingness to bring to these habits a calm, clear mindfulness has the power to open the door to new pathways of response, speech, choice, and ways of relating. The present, unencumbered by the past, becomes simpler, more accessible, and free.

11/7/20

The Middle Way

In the story of Siddhartha's journey of awakening, after leaving his palace of luxury, security, and pleasure, he commenced an ascetic path of meditation that involved complex practices of severe austerity. Punishing his body almost to the point of death, he found himself recalling a time in his childhood when he sat beneath the shade of a tree, watching the farmers tend their fields. He remembered the quiet contentment and happiness found in the simplicity of that moment. Nothing special was happening; the birds were singing, the sun shining, his mind and body were at ease, yet that moment was filled with a powerful sense of "enough." Nothing lacking, nothing to be added, nothing needed—simply seeing, listening, being, and a profound happiness and stillness. It was a powerful memory, reminding him that simplicity of peace did not lie in another dimension, nor could it be gained through mortifying or manipulating his body or his world.

The recollection of this simple peace was the beginning of his search for a "middle way"—not one rooted in avoidance or gain, denial or ambition, but through turning a wholehearted attention to shine upon this moment and discover the freedom he longed for. We need to find the "middle way" in our own lives. It is the art of finding balance. Reflecting upon our lives, we soon discover what serves us well—nurturing calmness, ease, and simplicity. We also discover what it is that leads to entanglement, confusion, distress, and anxiety. Wisdom is being able to discern the difference, then knowing what we need to nurture and what we need to learn to let go. Foolishness is the belief that we can continue treading the same, familiar pathways of confusion and complexity, hoping that at some point they will lead to a different outcome.

The Buddha said, "This is the path of happiness leading to the highest happiness and the highest happiness is peace." He never said that the path of meditation was a path of misery in pursuit of greater misery; it is a path dedicated to the discovery of peace in each moment. To understand this deeply, we are called upon to reconsider our understanding of true happiness. Happiness is more than the roller coaster highs we experience through excitement, success, or gain. We all encounter these moments in our lives and they bring a delight to be savored and appreciated. But they also remind us to discover a deeper happiness that is not dependent upon such circumstances. Happiness that is dependent on pleasant experiences is a fragile happiness which can trigger an inner busyness that only thirsts for more sights, sounds, tastes, and experiences. Living a life governed by the pursuit of the pleasant experience and the avoidance of the unpleasant rarely leads to a sense of ease and simplicity but instead to a complex web of pursuit and avoidance. Once, when I was teaching a retreat for young children, we spent some time talking about the nature of wanting. I asked the group what they felt would happen if they went through their lives always wanting something more, never feeling that they had enough in their lives to be happy. There were a few quiet moments, then a five-year-old voice piped up, "Trouble."

Just as moments of delight will touch our lives and hearts, we will also be asked to respond to encounters with loss, failure, blame, and pain. There will be times when we are separated from those we love, face disappointed dreams, experience loneliness and tension, or are hurt by others. Can we be at peace with all these moments? Can we find a simple, clear understanding within our hearts vast enough to embrace the variety of our experiences? Speaking to a community of monks and nuns, the Buddha said, "Any monk or nun can be at peace when showered with praise, kindness, and adoration. Show me the one who stays serene and balanced in the midst of harshness and blame; this is the monk or nun who is truly at peace." If we do not know peace in our hearts, it will elude us in all the areas of our lives. True peace is not a destination projected into the future, but a path and practice of the moment. Thich Nhat Hanh, the wonderful Zen teacher, once said, "Buddhism is a clever way of enjoying life. Happiness is available. Please help yourself."

Peace is not the absence of the unpleasant or challenging in our lives. Peace is most often found in the absence of prejudice, resistance, and judgment. Learning to live with simplicity does not mean that nothing difficult, unpleasant, or challenging will happen to us. Meditation is not an attempt to armor ourselves against life's realities. Instead, it is about learning to open, to discover a heart as vast as the ocean that can embrace the calm and the turbulence, the driftwood and the sparkling waves. Peace is not a denial of life but the capacity to be whole-heartedly with each moment, just as it is, without fear or avoidance. We learn to simplify, to strip away our expectations and desires, to let go of our fears and projections, and see the simple truth of each moment. Out of this simplicity is born an understanding and wise responsiveness that manifests in our speech, actions, and choices. We discover what it means to embrace our lives.

A woman once came to me wanting to be taught how to meditate. She was understandably distressed by the tension, struggle, and conflicting demands present in her life—financial hardship, an alcoholic partner, and a hostile stepson. She said, "All I want is some peace." After receiving some instructions she went home to practice only to return a week later even more distressed. She spoke of how, as her mind began to calm down, she became even more acutely aware of the nature of the conflicts in her life and what she would be called upon to change to bring the tension to an end. Puzzled, because it seemed that the meditation was indeed working, I asked her what the problem was. She answered, "I didn't ask for awareness, I only wanted peace."

Awareness and understanding have real implications in our lives. We need to be willing to be changed by the insights that come to us. When we recognize our habitual pathways of complexity, we are invited to find new pathways to travel.

Understanding the rhythm of change, the beginnings and endings intrinsic to life, is an insight that invites us to let go more easily. To try to hold onto, maintain, or preserve anything in this life, inwardly or outwardly, is to invite the experiences of deprivation, anxiety, and defensiveness into our hearts. Learning to embrace and live in harmony with all the changes, the births and deaths, beginnings and endings that life will inevitably bring to each of us, is to invite stillness and serenity into our hearts.

Simplicity is a journey that involves both our inner and outer worlds—they are interconnected, endlessly informing each other. Our lives are simply our hearts and minds taking form, made manifest. Our words, thoughts, actions, and choices are born within our hearts and minds. Untangling the knots of complexity found within our thoughts, feelings, and perceptions, we learn to untangle the knots of our lives. We learn how to be at home in each moment with calmness, balance, and the willingness to learn. Simplicity is not passive, a benign detachment from the turbulence of life; it is a way of placing our finger upon the pulse of our life and discovering the ways of liberation.

Patience and Compassion

In the *Tao Te Ching* it is said,

I have just three things to teach:
Simplicity, patience, and compassion.

These three are your greatest treasures.
Simple in actions and in thought,
You return to the source of being.
Patient with both friends and enemies,
You accord with the way things are.
Compassionate toward yourself,
You reconcile all beings in the world.

We carry with us the habits of a lifetime. We are not asked to unravel them all in one instant, but to care for and understand just one moment at a time; attuning ourselves to just this moment we begin to understand what leads to distress, complexity, and conflict, and what leads to calmness, balance, and freedom. Patience is the foundation of discovering simplicity. Patience is a gesture of profound kindness. We all have moments when we stumble and lose ourselves in our stories, fears, and fantasies. And we can all begin again in the next moment, recovering a sense of balance and openness. Patience teaches us to seek an inner refuge of simplicity, balance, and sensitivity in even the most turbulent moments. It is about learning to be a good friend to ourselves. Blame, judgment, and avoidance only divorce us from ourselves and exile us from the moment. Impatience always leads us away from where we are; wanting to jump into a better, more perfect moment. Impatience is the manifestation of resistance and aversion, it is the face of non-acceptance. Impatience never leads to the calm, simple contentment of being, but to perpetual restlessness and frustration. Patience is one of life's great arts, a lesson we learn not just once, but over and over. In the moments we find ourselves leaning into a future that has not arrived, we can pause and learn to stand calmly in the moment. When we find ourselves frustrated with ourselves or another, we can remember that this is the very moment we are invited to soften our resistance and open our hearts.

Once I found myself in a monastery filled with a burning motivation to practice meditation and be silent. Contrary to my expectation, the monastery was no oasis of peace and serenity but a construction site. The sounds of saws and hammers, scaffolding being erected, and trucks arriving with building materials permeated every corner. Radios played, dogs barked: clearly the value I placed on silence was not shared by others. In despair and frustration I found myself demanding of the abbot how I was supposed to meditate in the midst of this chaos. His answer was, "How can you not?"

We gladly turn our attention to those most significant of questions, "What is truly important to us in our lives? What do we truly value in this moment?" Holding these questions clearly, we discover that we want to be happy, to be free from struggle and separation. They are questions that return us to this moment, to ask ourselves, "Where is peace, where is freedom, where is simplicity in this moment?" Patient not just outwardly with the circumstances of our lives, but with the friends and enemies within ourselves, we learn the happiness and simplicity of being with what is.

Compassion is another essential companion on the journey to simplicity. Simplicity is not only a gift of compassion for ourselves, but also for the world. Deprivation, poverty, and hardship will not be eased by ever more strategies, councils, or prescriptions. As Gandhi once said, "There is enough in the world for everyone's needs, but not enough for everyone's greed." Each moment we lay down the burden of endless need, we become a conscious participant in easing the sorrow of the world. When we are no longer guided by the inexhaustible thirst of wanting, our relationship to life is guided by integrity. Compassion for ourselves is found in letting go of the stress of separation from the possibilities of richness, harmony, and freedom that lie within. Thomas Merton once said:

> Of what avail is it if we can travel to the moon,
> If we cannot cross the abyss that separates us from ourselves,
> This is the most important of all journeys
> And without it all of the rest are useless.

In Japan there is a monastic tradition whose practice is not only composed of traditional meditation but also the service of cleaning the local villages and public conveniences. Each morning the monks and nuns board their buses with buckets and mops to begin another day of cleaning toilets, streets, and waiting rooms. It is held as a sacred task, an act of thanksgiving, of caring for the world. When questioned on the spiritual value they found in such work, one of the nuns answered, "We are learning to live a simple life with great affluence."

Simplicity can be found nowhere else but the life we are in and the path we walk within it. It lives in our hearts and minds, awaiting our commitment and wholehearted attention. We do not create simplicity but rediscover its availability and possibility. We begin by being present, turning our attention to our lives and ourselves, and availing ourselves of the invitation offered in each moment to discover peace and freedom. It may be one of the most challenging journeys we make; we only travel it one step at a time. Responding to one of his ardent admirers, standing beneath the roof of the Sistine Chapel, Michaelangelo reportedly said, "If you only knew how much effort it took to get here, you wouldn't be so amazed."

GUIDED MEDITATION

Take a few moments in your day to be still. Relax your body, close your eyes, and listen inwardly. Bring a calm, gentle awareness to whatever appears in your mind. Be aware of what your thoughts revolve around and dwell upon most frequently. It might be the memory of an event or conversation that has been disturbing. It might be rehearsals or plans for the future. You might be aware of your mind obsessing about or judging yourself or another. You might be aware of a tension in your mind or body; a restless energy that is wanting something more than the simplicity of this moment.

The sticky, repetitive places our thoughts return to are messengers asking for our attention. What is being asked of us to release us from the complexity or confusion of this moment? Where does peace and calmness lie? Is there someone we need to forgive. Is there something we are being asked to let go of?

Can we nurture a greater generosity of heart or compassion for ourselves or another? Ask yourself,

■ "Where does simplicity lie in this moment?"

Hold this question with a patient receptivity but without demanding an answer. Listen to the responses that arise within you. The release from complexity, the peace and calmness we seek for, will be found within those responses.

renunciation

When my house burned down I gained
an unobstructed view of the moonlit sky

ZEN

RENUNCIATION is the unwavering companion of simplicity. A life dedicated to depth and compassion invites us to let go of the layers of relentless need and thirst to accumulate that can govern our lives, and to understand the insecurities and anxieties that separate us from ourselves and others. Renunciation is the greatest of all kindnesses—it teaches us not to lean upon anything that can crumble; it teaches us about genuine richness and freedom.

Some years ago I went into a Thai monastery for a period of retreat. The first morning I took my seat in the meditation hall and waited for the teacher to arrive with instructions on how to meditate. I waited and waited. On the third day I summoned up the courage to ask the abbot, "What should I be doing when I sit on a cushion?" expecting to receive a complex formula of meditation instructions. He looked at me with a puzzled expression on his face before answering, "Sit down and let go."

Can the heart of a meditative path be so simple—to sit down and let go? The lessons of simplicity teach us to love deeply and to let go; to savor each sound, taste, sight, and smell and to let go; to cherish each moment as a precious gift and to let go; to appreciate with profound sensitivity each connection with others, every thought and feeling, every birth and death, and to be a calm presence and conscious participant in their natural unfolding and passing. The path of simplicity is learning to live in harmony with the rhythms of life and each moment. It is a path of joy and freedom.

Hearing the word "renunciation" we may find our hearts quivering with fear and resistance. Images of ourselves as homeless and bereft, deprived of comfort and drowning in loneliness, pass through our minds. Renunciation may be equated with vulnerability and loss, a life of passivity and meaninglessness. We are faced with one of our deepest anxieties, of not knowing how we would define ourselves or find meaning without our array of possessions, opinions, beliefs, roles, and achievements. Culturally, we are encouraged to believe that possession, attainment, and achievement are the pathways to happiness. In the quest for simplicity we are invited to entertain another paradigm: that it is this very craving, holding, and possessiveness which brings complexity, confusion, and sorrow, and that renunciation is the mother of joy, simplicity, and freedom.

Complexity and entanglement have many sources in our lives. One of the main causes lies in the fear of losing what we have and the anxiety of not having enough. In fear of solitude and loneliness, we fill our lives and minds with distractions and busyness. Personal productivity has become the mantra of our time, the idea of stillness and simplicity terrifying—a sign of apathy or aimlessness. In the rush to be occupied endlessly and in the pursuit of stimulation, we neglect the quality of life, forget the simple joys of listening to the song of a bird, the laugh of a child, and the richness of one step taken with complete attention. George McDonald said:

> Work is not always required of a person
> There is such a thing as Sacred Idleness,
> The cultivation of which is now
> Fearfully neglected.

We may dream of a time when we can lie down beneath the night sky and do nothing but be present in its vastness with total attention. But our dreams are too often sabotaged by the busyness generated by anxiety. We seek evidence of our worth through what we produce, become, and surround ourselves with. Boredom has come to be regarded as one of our greatest enemies and we flee from it by generating endless complexity and busyness. Boredom may be no more than a surrender of sensitivity, yet, rather than turning our hearts and minds to rediscover that lost sensitivity, we thirst for even more exciting experiences, drama, and intensity. A young man about to bungee jump into the Grand Canyon was asked why he was engaging in such a perilous act. He answered, "These are the moments that shatter the boredom of living." When alienated from inner vitality we mistake intensity for wakefulness.

In the search for calm simplicity it is important for us to remember our dreams of intimacy, stillness, and happiness; to value their discovery. We may need to remember that boredom is a state of mind and not an accurate description of reality. A meditation master listening to his student's complaint of being bored, advised, "If you find something boring for ten minutes, stay with it for twenty minutes. If it's still boring do it for an hour. Stay present until you know what it means to be alive."

Some time ago the keepers at the Bronx Zoo became concerned when Gus the polar bear was observed swimming repetitively back and forth in his pool for hours on end. Animal psychologists and experts were consulted and the conclusion was that Gus was bored. Not that Gus wasn't somewhat aggrieved at living in New York rather than bounding through snowdrifts, or may have missed his freedom; boredom was the problem that needed solving rather than the issue of Gus's captivity. The solution—fill his pool with toys and distractions. As one keeper stated, "Hey, it works for us."

The times when we feel most discontented are the times when our minds flee most readily to the past or future in search of guarantees, control, and safety. Inner complexity is easy to identify—the mind swirls with a burden of thoughts, images, anxiety, speculation, and obsession. The feeling of "I can't let go" is a painful one. Seeking to end the pain of being trapped in our own turmoil, we make confused and desperate choices that lead to greater entanglement. Feeling adrift and fragmented, we search for happiness in the world of people, things, and fantasy, and find ourselves falling into familiar pits of frustration and discord.

The young Prince Siddhartha left the comfort and security of his palace and family to lead a homeless life, in search of enduring happiness and freedom. The homeless life is often praised as being the model of greatest renunciation. For many of us it is a much greater renunciation to discover what it really means to be at home in ourselves. To commit ourselves to being at home in our bodies, minds, hearts, and life, asks us to renounce the habit of abandoning ourselves and the moment. We often practice a kind of unconscious renunciation and homelessness—fleeing from where we are into the past or future and into the disconnected world of our daydreams and fantasies. To renounce the inclination to flee may be the greatest of all renunciations.

We find simplicity in our hearts and lives through paying attention to the roots of our complexity and then letting go. Albert Einstein advised, "Out of clutter, find simplicity. From discord, find harmony. In the middle of difficulty lies opportunity." Simplicity does not rely on divorcing ourselves from the world or on adopting a path of austerity, but on a careful examination of our relationship to the acquisitions, opinions, objects, and dreams which crowd our lives. We bring a simple question into this maze of complexity: "What leads to happiness and what leads to complexity and confusion?"

Baker Roshi, an American Zen master, said that the definition of an enlightened person is that they always have what they need. Whether sitting alone on a mountain, or in the middle of a crowd, there is no sense of anything being absent or lacking. Each moment, each situation, and each encounter offers everything that is needed for deepening sensitivity, compassion, peace, and understanding as long as we are paying attention. The mind calms, we step back a little from the forces of craving and aversion and turn our attention to this moment, discovering our capacity to be delighted by all that is before us.

Releasing Anxiety

We live in a culture that trains us to believe that we never have enough of anything and that we always need more in order to be happy. This is a training in anxiety and complexity. In the Tibetan Buddhist tradition there is depicted a realm of beings called "hungry ghosts" who sadly inhabit bodies with enormous stomachs yet whose throats are as narrow as needles. Unable to satisfy their appetite, they desperately roam the world in search of gratification. Trained in anxiety and complexity, we come to believe that life is made meaningful by possessing more, gaining more, and achieving more; protecting ourselves from loss and deprivation by holding on to all that we gain as tightly as possible.

Every year my insurance salesman visits me to assess my various insurance policies. Of course, his unspoken agenda is to persuade me to purchase more insurance cover. With a smile on his face he begins a long discourse on the unspeakable terrors and tragedies that may befall me. What if you had no work? What if you or your partner contracted a terminal illness? What if your children were in an accident? The list of possible disasters seems endless. Listening to him my eyes grow wider and wider, yet I also glimpse the bottomless chasm of fear I could inhabit if I lived by the rules of "what if?" The choice seems simple: do I choose to make fear my companion in life or do I choose to live with trust and skillful means?

We tend to believe that there will always be a better moment for us to find simplicity and happiness than the moment we are in. We cling tightly to all that we have and want, not seeing that this desperate holding and wanting only generates greater depths of fear. We look upon the world as an enemy or thief, intent upon depriving us of all we have accumulated. There is a story of an elderly, cantankerous man, miserly with everything including his love and trust, who awoke one night to find his house on fire. Climbing to the roof for safety, he looked down to see his sons holding a blanket for him to jump into. "Jump, father, jump, we'll save you," they called. He answered, "Why should I believe you? What do you want in return?" "Father, this is no time for arguments. Either jump or you'll lose your life." "I know you boys," he shouted, "lay the blanket on the ground and then I'll jump."

We believe that it is difficult to let go but, in truth, it is much more difficult and painful to hold and protect. Reflect upon anything in your lives that you grasp hold of—an opinion, a historical resentment, an ambition, or an unfulfilled fantasy. Sense the tightness, fear, and defensiveness that surrounds the grasping. It is a painful, anxious experience of unhappiness. We do not let go in order to make ourselves impoverished or bereft. We let go in order to discover happiness and peace. As Krishnamurti once said, "There is a great happiness in not wanting, in not being something, in not going somewhere."

In the search for simplicity we are drawn to ask ourselves: "What is truly lacking in this moment?" Would even more thoughts, possessions, experiences, sights, or sounds have the power to liberate us from complexity and unhappiness, or would they add more clutter to an over-cluttered life and heart? When we are lost in these states of want and need, contentment, simplicity, and peace feel far away. We become fixated upon the next moment, the moment we arrive at the rainbow's end, fulfilling our desires and gratifying our needs. The promise of happiness and peace is projected into the perfect moment, the ideal relationship, the next attainment or exciting experience. Although experience tells us how easily we become dissatisfied, bored, and disinterested with what we gain, we continue to invest our happiness and well-being in this projected promise.

Pursuing our obsessions, we forget that this acute sense of deprivation is not rooted in the world but in our own minds.

Simplicity is not concerned with resignation or passivity, nor with surrendering vision and direction in our lives. It is about surrendering our obsessions and addictions, and all the anxiety and unhappiness they generate. Over and over we learn to ask ourselves, "What is truly lacking in this moment?"

In my early years of meditation practice I had a great longing for stillness, believing that my progress depended on finding the perfectly quiet mind. I found myself pursuing the perfectly quiet world, believing it to be a precondition for the quiet mind. First I had a room in a tiny village, but soon became dissatisfied. The sound of an occasional truck or a market peddler disturbed whatever quiet I managed to find. So I moved further up the mountain to a small house, convinced that it would be perfect. Before long I was irritated by the sounds of passing herdsmen and the occasional barking of a dog, so once more I moved further up the mountain to an isolated hut, far removed from any human contact. I covered the windows with blankets so even the sun wouldn't distract me and I breathed a sigh of relief—perfect quiet. In that part of India lived tribes of large, silver-haired monkeys and they discovered the delight of my tin roof. One day, finding myself outside shouting and pouring abuse upon the monkeys, it finally occurred to me that perfect calm was perhaps more a state of mind than a state of environment.

Fixated upon getting, possessing, and arriving at the "perfect moment," we overlook the fact that the perfect moment comes to depend upon the fulfillment of our goals, desires, and fantasies. We believe we will be happy when we have ordered the world to suit our wants, expectations, and ambitions. Strangely, this perfect moment and promise of fulfillment never arrives; it is ceaselessly pushed over into the future as yet another need or desire arises within us. One of the richest men in America, after finally reaching his goal of possessing three billion dollars, remarked to a friend, "You know, I really don't feel all that secure. Maybe if I had four billion." Peace and simplicity are not so complicated; they are born of being, not of having. Each time we become lost in our obsessions and cravings we deprive ourselves of the simplicity, contentment, and freedom that is to be found in a single moment embraced with attention and the willingness to be touched by its richness. An ancient Sufi saying tells us, "Within your own house swells the treasure of joy, so why do you go begging from door to door?"

Renunciation is Compassion

One of my first teachers once told me, "Letting go is an act of compassion for yourself." We drive ourselves into deep states of sorrow and anxiety in our quest for gratification and happiness. Driven by what the Buddha described as the two deepest fears of a human being: the fear of having nothing and the fear of being no-one, we try to grasp the ungraspable, preserve the changing, secure the unpredictable, and guarantee the unknowable. It is an act of great kindness to learn how to let go in this life, to be with what is, to harmonize ourselves with life's inevitable changes, and open up to the mystery of the unknown. When we no longer live in fear of losing what we have, we can begin to learn how to love and appreciate what is already with us. We learn to reclaim our inner authority, to discover happiness within ourselves and within each moment. In a path of renunciation, all that we are truly letting go of is a world of unease and discontent. Coco Chanel once remarked, "How many cares one loses when one decides not to be something but to be someone."

In his first discourse, the Buddha stated that craving is the cause of sorrow and pain. The craving to gain what we do not have, the craving to get rid of what we do not want, and the craving for experience and identity, are all manifestations of an energy that leads us to depart from the truth of what is in each moment. The Buddha went on to say that the cause of sorrow lies in our own hearts and minds; the cause of happiness lies in our own hearts and minds. Our immediate response may be to say that this is too simplistic. There appear to be so many things that cause us sorrow—the job we dislike, the relatives we struggle with, the aches in our body; the list is endless. As we look more deeply we should ask: do any of these hold the power to cause us to be lost in sorrow, pain, or confusion? Or is it the movements of our minds that dismiss, judge, reject, and avoid, which cause the greatest pain and sorrow?

We can go through life with the mantra, "This shouldn't be happening. I want something else to happen. This should be different than it is." Pursuing what we want and do not have, trying to get rid of what we have and don't want, losing interest in what previously fascinated us, are all the tentacles of a single energy of craving. It is a powerful energy that leads us to flee from the moment and ourselves. As our appetites become jaded, we find ourselves needing ever more intense excitement and experience. The Buddha compared this energy of craving to a forest fire which consumes the very ground that sustains it. Our energy, time, well-being, and peace are consumed in the fires of craving. Renunciation, learning to let go gently and clearly in our lives, extinguishes the fire; it is the antidote to craving.

In the last century an affluent tourist went to visit a Polish rabbi, renowned for the depth of his learning and compassion. Arriving at the impoverished village where the rabbi made his home, he was astonished to discover the rabbi living in a simple room with only a few books and the most basic furniture. "Rabbi, where is all your furniture, your library, your diplomas?" he asked. "Where are yours?" answered the rabbi. "Mine? But I am only a visitor here." "So am I," replied the rabbi.

In the early 70s I traveled to India in search of a spiritual path and found myself in a Tibetan refugee village. I found a community of people who had lost so much: their country, their homes, their possessions, and their families. What was so stunning was the absence of despair, rage, hatred, and desire for vengeance. Their openhearted welcome and generosity, the smiles upon their faces, the devotion that permeated the camp, were a testimony to the reality that they had not lost their heart.

There is a sacred hunger rooted in our hearts—a yearning for freedom, happiness, connectedness, and peace. It is a hunger that prevents us from surrendering to despair and disconnection, that inspires us to continue searching for a way of feeling truly intimate in this world, at one with life, free from conflict and sorrow. In our confusion, this sacred hunger becomes distorted and diverted; it turns into craving and the pursuit of projected promise invested in experience and things outside ourselves.

Renunciation is not a dismissal of the world. It does not involve surrendering the joy found in all the precious and delightful impressions and experiences that will visit us in this life. Through withdrawing the projected promise invested in sensation, impression, and experience, we learn to find a sense of balance that embraces the pleasant, unpleasant, and neutral experience. Believing that happiness and fulfillment lie outside of ourselves we project onto the 10 thousand objects and experiences in this life the power for them to devastate, enrage, gratify, or elate us. We then become a prisoner of those 10 thousand things. Withdrawing this projected promise, we can deeply appreciate the pleasant, remain steady in the midst of the unpleasant, and be fully sensitive to the neutral impressions and experiences life brings. We discover that the root of happiness lies not in what we are experiencing but how we are experiencing it. It is the withdrawal of the projected promise and the surrender of the fear of deprivation which enables a relationship to life that is rooted in sensitivity, compassion, and intimacy. Craving propels us outwardly, away from ourselves and from this moment, into an endless quest for certainty and identity. By exploring the energy of craving and loosening its hold, we are returned to ourselves, able to acknowledge the sacred hunger within us for intimacy and awakening. At ease within ourselves, we discover a profound refuge and happiness rooted in our own capacities for awareness and balance.

The Enlightened and the Unenlightened

The Buddha spoke about the distinction between an enlightened and an unenlightened person. Both the enlightened and the unenlightened experience feelings, sensations, sounds, sights, and events that can be pleasant, unpleasant, or neutral. When an unenlightened person encounters the unpleasant experience they grieve, lament, and become distraught and distracted. Two levels of sorrow are experienced; one in the actual experience and one in the reactions and story about it. It is as if a person crossing the pathway of an archer was shot by an arrow; whether enlightened or unenlightened, that person would experience pain. The difference lies in the level of both the story and the fear that are added to the experience. In seeing the archer prepare to shoot a second arrow, the unenlightened person would already be anticipating its pain, building a story centered around living with a wounded leg and entertaining thoughts of anger towards the archer. In the heart of the unenlightened person, layers of aversion and associations with the past and future lead them to depart from the reality of what is actually being experienced in that moment. The unpleasant experience is layered with aversion and resistance. We try to end the unpleasant experience by finding one that is more pleasant or by suppressing or avoiding it. In the midst of any of the unpleasant experiences, we need to ask ourselves what is more painful, the actual experience or the stories, fear, and resistance with which we surround it. Calm simplicity does not depend upon the annihilation or control of the unpleasant experience but is born of our willingness to let go of the layers of our stories and fears.

The enlightened person is not exempt from any form of feelings, whether pleasant, unpleasant or neutral, but is not bound or governed by them. The arrow will hurt, but the pain of the body will not be matched by sorrow and struggle in the mind. Blame, judgment, and retaliation are the children of fear. Wise responsiveness, equanimity, and discriminating wisdom are the children of deep understanding. The enlightened person would find little value in shouting, "This is unfair" at the world, would not seek to take revenge upon the archer nor vow to never venture out again. The enlightened person knows the pathways of wise response rather than blind reaction. Surrendering the story is not a dismissal of the wounded leg but is an empowerment, releasing the capacity to care for what needs to be cared for with compassion and responsiveness, letting go of all the extra layers of fear, apprehension, and blame.

The pleasant experience evokes a different response and different story line in us. We want more, we don't want it to end, we strategize the ways to defend it—it is layered with craving and grasping. We have a moment of calm during meditation and find ourselves rehearsing our debut as the next world-famous teacher. A smile from a colleague and in our minds we are already embroiled in the romance of the century. Once more our stories divorce us from the simplicity of the moment and we are puzzled and disappointed when these stories are frustrated. Pleasant experiences are hijacked by craving and wanting, and once more we are not living in the simplicity of the moment but in the dramas of our minds. In the midst of the pleasant experience, we can learn to let go of our stories, projections, and fantasies. We can learn to love what is.

The neutral experiences, sounds, sights, and sensations we encounter become layered with voices of confusion that tell us that something is missing, something needs to be added. If the things of this world neither delight nor threaten us they are often dismissed, ignored, or simply missed. The tree outside our window, made familiar by time, no longer appears to offer anything to attract our attention. We fail to notice the texture of its leaves, its changing colors, its growing and aging, the way the sun reflects on its leaves. We believe we need something more stimulating and exciting for it to be worthy of our attention. In learning to stay in the present, we discover that it is the power of our attention that makes all things worthy.

There are experiences of pain that are inevitable in this life, rooted in our bodies as they age or sicken. In our lives we will all experience loss, separation, and contact with those who threaten us. There are levels of sorrow and pain that are optional, rooted in fear, aversion, and grasping. We need to learn to let go of the stories that carry our fears and wanting, we need to learn to see life, ourselves, others, as they actually are. Simplicity is always available. Learning to let go of the layers of our stories and cravings, learning to let go of our craving for the pleasant and our aversion for the unpleasant, is the discovery of peace.

In the Tao it is said, "In the pursuit of knowledge, every day something is gained. In the pursuit of freedom, every day something is let go of." We tend to hold grandiose ideas of renunciation, regarding it as a spiritually heroic task or break-through experience on our path that will happen at some future time. A spiritual life asks us to hold onto nothing—not our opinions, beliefs, judgments, past, nor dreams of the future. It seems a formidable task but we are not asked to do it all at once. Life is a journey of 10 thousand renunciations, sometimes in a single day. We are not asked to be an expert, but always a beginner. The only moment we can let go is the moment we are present in.

The Wisdom of Impermanence

As we reflect upon the nature of life and ourselves, we discover that there is an innate naturalness to letting go. The nature of all life is change; winter lets go its hold to change into spring; for summer to emerge spring must end and this season can only last for a time before it fades into autumn, which in turn lets go for winter to emerge once more. In the same way, our infancy was let go of as we emerged into our childhood. All of our life transitions, our capacity to grow and mature, depend upon a natural process of letting go of what went before. No matter how strenuous our efforts, we cannot make one single thing last. No matter how much we delight in a pleasant thought, experience, or connection, we cannot force it to stay. No matter how much we dislike or fear an experience or impression, it is already in the process of changing into something else. There is a remarkable simplicity discovered as we harmonize our own life with the natural story of all life, which is change. From the moment of our birth, our life has been teaching us about letting go. There is remarkable complexity in seeking to bend and mold life's story to support our personal agendas of craving and aversion. We are not separate in any way from the process of change, not just detached observers. We are part of this life with all of its seasons and movements.

Aitken Roshi, a much beloved Western Zen master, once said, "Renunciation is not getting rid of the things of this world, but accepting that they pass away." A deep understanding of impermanence is an insight that has the power to transform our lives. Understanding the nature of change deeply and unshakably loosens the hold of craving and aversion, bringing calmness and great simplicity. To study life is to study impermanence. This insight into impermanence is not a breakthrough experience but an ongoing exploration of what is true. Take a walk through the rooms of your home—can you find one single thing that is eternal, that is not already in a process of change? Explore your body—it speaks to you of the inevitable process of aging and change. Walk through the rooms of your mind with its cascade of thoughts, plans, anxieties, memories, and images. Can you hold on to any of them? Can you decide only to have pleasant thoughts or ideas, only pleasant feelings or sensations? Neither sorrow nor complexity are born of this changing world, but of our grasping and aversion, and our desire to seek the unchanging in anything that is essentially changing. As you take those walks through the rooms of your life and mind, ask yourself whether anything you encounter truly holds the power to dictate your happiness or sorrow, or whether it is more true that the source of happiness and sorrow lies within your own heart and mind.

When we hear the word "impermanence" we tend to nod our heads wisely in agreement—it is an obvious truth. Yet, when caught in craving or aversion, we suffer bouts of amnesia, convinced that everything is impermanent except this experience, feeling, or thought. Life continues to be our greatest teacher, penetrating these moments of forgetfulness, if we are willing to listen and pay attention. In truth, there is no choice but to let go; the nature of impermanence tells us that no matter how desperately we hold onto anything, it is already in the process of leaving us. Our choice is whether or not we suffer in the course of meeting the inevitable arrivals and departures, the beginnings and endings, held in every moment of our lives. Each time we are lost in craving or aversion, we open the door to a flood of thoughts, stories, strategies, and images. Each time we learn to let go, we open the door to peace and simplicity, to joy and appreciation.

Renunciation is not a spiritual destination, nor a heroic experience dependent upon great striving and will. Renunciation is a practice of kindness and compassion undertaken in the midst of the small details and intense experiences of our lives. It is the heart of meditation practice. We learn to sit down and let go. Each time we return our attention to the breath or to the moment we are in, we are practicing renunciation. In that moment we have let go of the pathways of stories and speculation about what is happening, and have turned our attention to what is actual and true in each moment. The practice of renunciation is essentially a celebration of simplicity.

A group of businessmen renowned for their dishonesty went to visit a great Indian saint, intent on earning the merit they hoped would balance their covetousness. Sitting down, they proceeded to sing her praises, extolling her great virtues of wisdom, renunciation, and simplicity. After listening for some minutes her face creased into a smile and she began to laugh. Disconcerted, the group asked what was so amusing to her. Answering she said, "It is not I who is the great renunciate, it is you, because you are living in such a way that you have renounced the truth."

Moment-to-Moment Renunciation

Letting go is a present moment practice. We learn to sit down and let go. We love deeply and let go. We embrace wholeheartedly the laughter and joy of our lives and let go. We meet the challenging, disturbing, and unpleasant, and let go. We are always beginners in the practice of renunciation. Each moment we begin we are following the pathways of freedom rather than the pathways of sorrow.

Studying life, we see the truth of the process of change from which nothing is exempt. Understanding this deeply we live in accord with its truth, and we live peacefully and simply. We liberate the world, other people, and ourselves to unfold and change according to our own rhythms, withdrawing our personal agendas rooted in craving and aversion. Letting go, we liberate ourselves from the burden of unfulfilled or frustrated desire. We learn to rest in ourselves and in each moment. Reflecting on impermanence, we begin to appreciate deeply the futility and unnecessary sorrow of being lost in craving or resistance.

Renunciation comes effortlessly to us in times of calm and ease. Nothing stops; sounds, sights, thoughts, and feelings all continue to arise and pass—seen and appreciated wholeheartedly. Yet none of them gains a foothold in our minds and hearts, our inner balance and well-being is undisturbed; there is a natural letting go. There are times in our lives when calm and balance seem to be a distant dream as we find ourselves lost in turmoil, struggle, or distress. In those moments we remember the freedom of being able to let go, yet the intensity of our struggle overwhelms us. In those moments, the first step towards peace is to recognize that we are lost. In those moments, it is not more thinking, analyzing, or struggle that is required; instead we are invited to look for simplicity. In these moments of complexity, letting go requires investigation, effort, and dedication—recognizing the sorrow of being entangled.

The Buddha spoke of wise avoidance, a word that may carry for us associations of denial or suppression. There is a difference between wise avoidance and suppression. Suppression is the unwillingness to see; wise avoidance is the willingness to see but the unwillingness to *engage in* pathways of suffering.

In moments of intense struggle, renunciation happens in a different way; by learning to step out of the arena of contractedness. We turn our attention to the fostering of calm and balance. Bringing our attention into our body, to listening, to touching, to breathing, we learn to loosen the grip of struggle and confusion. Recovering a consciousness of expansiveness and balance, the understanding of the nature of our struggle comes more easily to us and we may discover we can let go.

It is easy to let go when there is nothing that we particularly crave or resist. Yet it is in the midst of our deepest obsessions and resistances that renunciation holds the power to transform our heart and world. Our capacity to let go is often clouded by ambivalence and reluctance. We know we suffer through overeating, but the second plate of food really does taste so good. We know that our anger towards another person makes us suffer, but if we were to let it go they may get away with the suffering they inflicted. We know that fantasy is a poor substitute for happiness, but its flavor is pleasurable. We know we may suffer through exaggerated ambition, but the feeling of pride when we attain our goals justifies the pain. Pleasure and happiness are too often equated with being the same; in reality they are very different. Pleasure comes. It also goes. It is the flavor and content of many of the impressions we encounter in our lives. Happiness has not so much to do with the content or impressions of our experiences; but with our capacity to find balance and peace amid the myriad impressions of our lives. Treasuring happiness and freedom, we learn to live our lives with openness and serenity. Not enslaved to the pleasant sensation, we no longer fear the unpleasant. We love, laugh, and delight, and hold onto nothing.

The appetite of craving arises from the pain of disconnection. The pain of believing ourselves to be incomplete or inadequate compels us to seek from the world all that we feel unable to offer ourselves. This pain of disconnection is not always acute; at times we describe it as boredom, forgetting that boredom is never a description of reality but a description of a state of mind superimposed upon reality. Boredom is often a surrender of sensitivity, clouding our capacity to see, listen to, and touch each moment as if we have never encountered it before. The antidote to boredom is not more sounds, sensations, and experiences, but recovering our capacity to see anew in each moment. The world we think we know, the people we think we know, the sounds and experiences we have encountered countless times before, come alive to us in new ways each moment we give them our wholehearted attention. Our storehouse of images, associations, history, and concepts is burned down in the light of compassionate, full attention.

Renunciation is not the territory of saints or ascetics but the territory of each one of us who treasures freedom. Each moment we let go, we embody freedom and follow the pathway of happiness. It is a present moment practice; every moment is the right moment to learn how to let go.

GUIDED MEDITATION

Take a few minutes to sit quietly, relax your body, close your eyes, and breathe out. Reflect for a moment upon the places in your mind and heart you visit the most often, yet feel to be the places of greatest sorrow or struggle. A failed relationship, a childhood hurt, a tension with another person, a frustrated hope. Be aware of the stickiness and tightness of these places, felt in your body, mind, and heart.

What is needed for you to be able to let go, to find a new beginning, to find peace? Is it forgiveness, compassion for yourself or another, tolerance, or understanding? How could you find simplicity in this moment?

Reflect upon the times of greatest happiness in your life—found in intimacy with another, moments of true appreciation and sensitivity in nature, times alone, a moment when you have felt that this moment is complete.

Be aware of what it is that opens the doors of appreciation, connection, and calm; that makes the expectation, fear, wanting, and distractedness fall away. Take some time to hold in your heart the question,

■ "What in this moment is lacking?"

integrity

> *Upon goodness of heart is built wise attention;*
> *upon wise attention is built liberating wisdom.*
>
> THE BUDDHA

In the midst of some of the darkest moments and most tormented events in human history there have emerged individuals who stun us with profound but simple acts of goodness. A homophobic inmate on death row reaches out to hold the hand of a prisoner dying of AIDS. A teenage monk, his body broken by torture, meditates to extend compassion to his torturer. A young girl, her body devastated by napalm burns, finds the generosity of heart to offer forgiveness to the pilot who dropped the bomb. In a single gesture, through a few words or simple acts of kindness, someone's world is transformed. Integrity is the gift of a wise and loving heart. There is no one whose life is not enriched by the kindness, respect, and compassion that finds its source in integrity. James Russell Lowell succinctly expressed it saying, "All the beautiful sentiments in the world weigh less than a single lovely action."

We may not find ourselves in desperate situations that ask for heroic actions. Integrity finds expression in the countless moments in our lives that invite us to interact with the world from a deep inner place of honesty, respect, and compassion. It is easier to be motivated by the wish for personal advantage, comfort, and gratification than to be guided by ethics and wisdom. Yet the healing of our planet, our communities, and our families asks us to find within ourselves the goodness of heart that seeks to protect and enrich, rather than to exploit or harm.

A life of simplicity, wisdom, and peace begins with an exploration of ethics. It is our personal ethics that shape how we live our lives, what we dedicate ourselves to, and how we interact with the world. Do we seek to gain rather than to give; do we shelter in dishonesty rather than find the courage of honesty; do we harbor resentment rather than explore our capacity to forgive? Ethical guidelines are an exploration of the landscape of our heart and mind, revealing to us the ways to inner simplicity and peace.

In the Buddhist tradition, the Buddha is portrayed seated upon a lotus flower. The lotus blossom can be seen as a symbol of integrity, a natural wisdom of heart that supports the emergence of wisdom. Lotus flowers never grow in water that is too sterile or clean, but are rooted in the dark, muddy depths of ponds. For most of us, a genuine sense of integrity is rooted in an intentional and gentle exploration of the darker waters of our own hearts. We all hold within us the capacity to cause harm and to bring about the end of harm. Our propensity towards greed, vanity, craving, and anger lives side by side our capacity for generosity, love, compassion, and patience. It is our willingness to embrace all these inner dimensions that allows genuine integrity to emerge, the lotus flower to bloom.

Through understanding the painfulness of greed we are moved to be generous. Through our experience of the suffering caused by hatred and divisiveness, we are moved to discover the source of love and forgiveness. In our willingness to turn our attention towards the shadows in our own hearts and lives, we find an integrity that is true and unshakeable. An ethical life is not a *state* of sanctity that we arrive at, but a verb; we discover genuine integrity in those significant moments when we follow the pathway of ending harm and sorrow rather than causing it.

The exploration of integrity is the exploration of simplicity and freedom. It is integrity of heart that directly contributes to releasing us from the distress of guilt, regret, shame, and fear. The ethical guidelines of the Buddhist tradition are not intended to be a spiritual corset, burdening our lives with complex rules of right and wrong, good and bad, sin and grace. Adherence to rules alone can disguise unethical sentiments of moral superiority, self-righteousness, or fear. A truly ethical life is born of wisdom and *contributes* to wisdom; it is born of compassion and *embodies* compassion.

The conscious cultivation of a life of integrity is an indispensable piece in the mystery of awakening. In the monastic tradition of Buddhism, the nuns and monks accept more than two hundred ethical precepts, referred to as training guidelines, and these precepts shape the way in which they interact with the world. Laypeople are encouraged towards a simpler framework of only five or eight precepts. The numbers are to some extent irrelevant. What is of true significance is the commitment to the guidelines as a spiritual practice and a framework for living. It is a commitment that encourages us to bring sensitivity to our bodies, minds, and hearts, and to the ways we interact with the world of events, sights, sounds, people, and circumstances. It is also making a commitment to integrity, honesty, and respect in all the circumstances of our lives.

The Loving Kindness of Ethics

The Buddha described an ethical life as a heartfelt commitment to bodily acts of loving kindness, verbal acts of loving kindness, and mental acts of loving kindness. Genuine ethics are rooted in the deep treasuring of harmlessness, generosity, and the end of conflict and sorrow—loving kindness in its truest sense. They are the healers of division, mistrust, and fear, and they awaken our own capacity for freedom. In these commitments, the twin pillars of wisdom and compassion merge; they are the path of the Bodhisattva and the Buddha.

The ethical guidelines of the Buddhist tradition invite us to live a life of loving kindness, through restraint and cultivation.

We communicate with the world through our bodies, speech, and minds, and so we are encouraged to explore the intentions and forces that guide our words, actions, thoughts, and choices, appreciating the power they hold to impact on our world in each moment. The ethical guidelines, undertaken as a meditative practice, invite us to explore the origins of our actions, speech, and thought. We learn to return to the kindergarten of wisdom—the understanding of what leads to suffering and separation, and what leads to harmony and freedom. The essential lessons of compassion are learned in this kindergarten; we learn them not just once, but over and over. A Zen master was once asked, "What is the key to happiness?" He answered, "Good judgment." "How do I gain good judgment?" he was questioned. "Experience," was the reply. "How then do I get experience?" the student further probed. "Bad judgment," were his final words. Our teachers have been met in the countless experiences of our lives that teach us the ways of generating complexity and confusion, and the ways of cultivating simplicity and peace.

Each one of us encounters the moments when we leave the monastery, rise up off our meditation cushion, and enter the world where we act, speak, and interact. These moments of entry are some of the most important moments on our spiritual path. They are moments of possibility that invite the greatest mindfulness. Many students of meditation discover that with their eyes closed in meditation it is possible to discover refined and subtle depths of awareness that they seem to lose in a cascade of habit and reactivity the moment they leave their meditation cushion. A telephone call from a parent, a meeting with a colleague, Christmas dinner with the family, being stuck in rush hour traffic—these are the ordinary moments of our lives that often open the door to familiar patterns of judgment, self-centeredness, anger, and habit. What a difference it would make in those moments to remember our commitment to bodily, verbal, and mental acts of loving kindness. Lost in our habitual reactions, we build up inner storms of regret that feature the endless monologues of "if only" and "should." We judge ourselves and others harshly, and generate spirals of complexity in our hearts and minds. By renewing our commitment to integrity as we open our eyes at the close of our meditation, we bring with us into the world a practice that is alive and embodied.

Leaving to attend her first meditation retreat after a tense and fraught week at work, a woman drove for many hours through a snowstorm becoming increasingly anxious and stressed, only to plow her car into a snowdrift a few yards from the entrance to the center. Walking into the building, she saw a sign suggesting loving kindness and a milling crowd of people preoccupied with their own arrival arrangements, and she became even more distraught. Meeting one of the staff, she began to berate him for the weather, the road conditions, for almost every trauma she had experienced in her life. Asking for her keys, he offered to park her car and bring her bags to her room while she helped herself to dinner. After leaving the retreat she wrote to thank him, saying that that one single act of kindness had touched her so deeply she would never forget it. In our own lives, the simple gestures of respect, honesty, compassion, and care we receive from others serve to remind us of the power of integrity; a capacity we all hold within ourselves.

Treasuring freedom and compassion, we cultivate an ethical life not as an end in itself, but as a means to serenity and wisdom. It is sometimes said that if you want to know about your past, look at your mind now. If you want to know about your future, look at your mind now. We sow the seeds of our future experience through what we commit ourselves to in this moment. There is a powerful relationship between integrity and simplicity. Dedicated to integrity, we are directly caring for the quality of our mind and heart, and of all life. The Buddha once said, "No one who truly loves themselves could ever harm another, for they would be harming themselves." A living integrity liberates us from the guilt-driven thinking that ensues from actions and speech born of habit or dishonesty. Each time we speak, act, or think in ways that harm or undermine others or ourselves, we are left with a residue of regret, fear, or guilt, that clouds our capacity to be present and awake. U Pandita, a forceful and beloved Burmese master, once said, "How can we expect to deepen in understanding if we do not live an ethical life? Living without integrity, we endlessly create the conditions for unpleasant mind states and feelings to arise." A commitment to integrity is a commitment to living a life without residues, a life of loving kindness and freedom. Words, thoughts, and actions of loving kindness and integrity leave no trace of regret in our minds and hearts. Stillness and calmness are the children of integrity; simplicity is the companion of integrity.

Cultivation and Restraint

The ethical guidelines in the Buddhist tradition include the pathways to restraint and cultivation. We learn to restrain harmful or unskillful patterns of body, speech, and mind—not because they are "bad" or "wrong," but because they lead to sorrow, confusion, and division. We learn to pause with mindfulness and care in the moments of such patterns so we can come to understand them and no longer be imprisoned by them. We welcome our shadow and demons and learn to befriend them, to explore all their textures and forms, and find a way of being in which they no longer compel us.

On the eve of the Buddha's enlightenment, the young prince Siddhartha took his seat beneath the branches of the Bodhi tree and in the first hours of the night was assailed by all the powers of Mara, the forces of delusion. Anger, greed, doubt, lust, envy, and fear all came to visit him. Siddhartha sat still, not denying or rejecting any of the faces of Mara. Neither did he panic, blame, or become agitated. Greeting Mara with a calm welcome, he responded, saying simply, "I know you." Our own capacity to understand, befriend, and investigate the shadows of unskillfulness and harmfulness that lie in our hearts is the beginning of our capacity to find freedom.

We learn to cultivate and nurture skillful, loving, and respectful responses of body, speech, and mind because they contribute to the happiness and freedom of all living beings. It takes great courage and steadfastness to live an ethical life in a world that has come to accept self-cherishing and self-gratification as a norm. It is a practice that demands an extraordinary alertness and dedication. Sometimes it asks us to extend ourselves beyond the boundaries of what is familiar and comfortable. Sometimes it involves taking risks as we venture into ways of relating that are not always applauded or encouraged by others. A woman described the jeers of derision and isolation she faced when she felt she could no longer engage in workplace practices of gossip and petty theft. A young man spoke of the rejection and judgment he received when he decided he could no longer collude in his community's support of their abusive teacher. Integrity involves not only making difficult choices in our lives, but also the capacity to make those choices without being judgmental of others.

Discriminating wisdom is an integral part of nurturing liberating wisdom. Acceptance and tolerance in meditative paths can be confused with passivity or a blind condoning of unwholesomeness. Genuine acceptance, the balanced heart and mind that can see things as they are, does not imply that everything is acceptable. The prejudice, oppression, abuse, and violence that scar our families and communities is not changed by passivity or idealism, but through our own capacity to make wise choices in our engagements with the world around us and within us. The pain in our world will not be changed by the technical skills of observation we develop in our meditation, but through an inner commitment not to consent to the causes of pain.

Detachment does not mean disengagement, but the capacity to hold sorrow and joy with balance. A life of integrity is by nature an engaged life, consciously concerned with engendering well-being, freedom, and respect. Discriminating wisdom, rooted in our capacity to distinguish between what causes suffering and what ends suffering, is at the root of all ethical choices and acts. As Robert Louis Stevenson put it, "Everybody, sooner or later, sits down to a basket of consequences."

Harmlessness

Treasuring loving kindness and freedom, we commit ourselves to harmlessness. We refrain from endangering or harming any living creature through thought, word, or action. We dedicate ourselves to protecting the life, safety, and dignity of all living creatures. Most of us do not commit acts of extreme violence or cruelty, yet through carelessness, the desire for personal advantage, or habit, we may find ourselves harming another in our thoughts or actions. We may harbor thoughts of resentment, judgment, hatred, or envy. We may banish from our hearts those who have hurt us, or turn away from those who challenge us. We may find ourselves walking through our lives, leaving behind us a trail of hurt, fear, or mistrust. Restraint does not mean that feelings of anger, judgment, or resentment should never arise; they will and do arise. Restraint means having the willingness to acknowledge that we create both our mind and world through the manner in which we greet the arising of these feelings in the present. We can travel familiar pathways of bitterness, retaliation, and anger, or we can take a moment to pause and appreciate the consequences of traveling those pathways. Do we ever come out of a bout of bitterness feeling lighter, more connected, or happier? Or do we emerge as if from a nightmare, exhausted and undermined? Can we learn the possibilities that may be offered through walking the pathways of patience, tolerance, and loving kindness? These are the pathways of integrity and simplicity.

Refraining from endangering or harming any living being applies equally to ourselves. Through fear, feelings of inadequacy, or worthlessness, we are prone to addiction, submissiveness, self-judgment, and self-hatred. We undermine our sense of dignity, possibility, and innate worth through thoughts and actions of inner terrorism. Bodily, verbal, and mental acts of loving kindness are learned in the territory of our inner relationship. Sometimes we are undoing the habits of a lifetime, or legacies we have inherited from others, and we are asked to find depths of dedication, courage, and perseverance within ourselves. In our moments of self-harming, we also learn to pause, to remember the qualities of freedom, peace, and wisdom that are possible for each of us.

Integrity not only has a spiritual dimension but also a practical one embodied in the lifestyles we choose. We are participants in the world we live in—conscious and unconscious. Dedicated to loving kindness, we learn the wisdom of simplicity, mindfulness, and care. Through the countless small actions we engage in, the loving hand we reach out to another, the wants we let go of, the time we give to those who most need it, we change our world. A single step taken with mindfulness may mean the difference between the life and death of another living creature. A single thought of loving kindness may mean the difference between loneliness or a sense of being loved for the person before us. A single act of compassion may save another person from feelings of abandonment.

The Path of Generosity and Honesty

We refrain from taking anything that is not freely given to us. Again, most of us are not in the business of fraud, theft, or burglary. Cultivating true honesty is a daily challenge. In a culture that is increasingly individualistic, we are regularly presented with the philosophy of entitlement. We receive the messages that we are entitled to get what we want, to not endure discomfort; and are encouraged to believe that we will be deemed unsuccessful if we do not consciously pursue our needs, desires, and yearnings for gratification. A recent advertisement proclaimed, "You deserve it all." This is a philosophy which can engender subtle and gross dishonesty and greed. We are vulnerable to dishonesty as long as the source of happiness and well-being is projected outside of ourselves. Inner feelings of deprivation, poverty, and inadequacy are not determined by how much or how little we have, but by our exile from genuine inward happiness. Integrity is cultivated in the countless moments in our lives that may be governed by a sense of need and want. With loving kindness we learn to pause and appreciate the consequences of taking or pursuing that which is not freely given—fear and unease follow, shame, and the uncomfortable awareness that there is little that we can gain that quenches our thirst for happiness. Simone de Beauvoir once said, "To be moral is to discover fundamentally one's own being." The conscious cultivation of integrity is an invitation to discover ourselves and the inner happiness that relies upon nothing.

In our commitment to integrity and freedom we consciously cultivate honesty and generosity. Honesty is what enables people to trust us, open up to us, and feel protected. In so many meditation centers and spiritual communities it is a collective commitment to honesty that engenders an environment of safety and trust. A hundred strangers gather together for extended periods of time; there are no locks on the doors, no security, no bars on the windows. It is a celebration of honesty and respect. Generosity with time, possessions, attention, and care, is born of the same quality of inner abundance and trust. True generosity is not the giving away of what no longer interests us or is not needed. True generosity is a way of stretching ourselves beyond the boundaries of personal comfort, advantage, and need. In the Tibetan tradition of Buddhism it is said, "The Bodhisattva has no boundaries." This does not imply that we should never say "No" or neglect ourselves. However, it does invite us to look at the source of generosity in our interactions with life.

Sexual Integrity

We refrain from sexual misconduct and harm. Cultivating bodily acts of loving kindness includes the sexual relationships we engage in. In the complex and volatile area of sexuality, mindfulness and integrity protect us from exploitation, disrespect, and fear. Lust appears to hold the power to blind us. When caught in the throes of infatuation, mindfulness, sensitivity, and balance are frequently forgotten. The power of craving, needing, and wanting becomes focused upon achieving specific goals of possession and gratification. Times of sexual infatuation may be some of the most concentrated moments in our lives, yet it is not a wise concentration. Tension, feelings of incompleteness, need, and dependency all make up the tapestry of sexual infatuation. Emerging from the trance of lust days or months later, we often find ourselves wondering what it was all about. The person we yearned for so desperately, who appeared so perfect and wondrous, now appears flawed.

Cultivating bodily acts of loving kindness, we approach sexual relationships aware of our intentions; we cultivate generosity and respect. We learn to step out of the compelling nature of our fantasies and needs, and acknowledge that meaningful sexual relationships are born of a shared commitment to understanding and freedom. We appreciate the power of our sexuality in its capacity to harm or as a vehicle through which love and generosity are communicated.

Wise Speech

We refrain from speaking words of harshness, dishonesty, or heedlessness. Words carry immense power to harm or heal. Wars are escalated through words, families divided, conversions undertaken, and prejudice perpetuated. Words in poems or stories inspire us, they soothe and comfort us when we're distressed, and they have the potential to communicate powerful insights. They are vehicles of communication and we are asked in our commitment to integrity to show care for what it is we are communicating.

In cultivating wise speech, we are invited to be aware of what is occurring within us in the moments before words are spoken. Before our words lies a complex landscape of feelings, memories, thoughts, and intentions. Within this landscape lurk the complexities of our personalities—the need to prove ourselves, to be admired, the fear of being visible to others, our insecurities, angers, and anxieties. As long as we are unconscious of this landscape, then our speech will also tend to be unconscious. Awareness is the forerunner of integrity. So often our speech has a compulsive nature; words fly from our mouths in ways that shock us. We make grand pronouncements, chatter, or find ourselves gossiping or judging others, and are left wondering, "Where did that come from?" The intensity and compelling force of our thoughts will often find its expression in the intensity and compelling nature of our speech. A commitment to integrity involves moving from unconsciousness to mindfulness, from habit to wise intention.

Unconsciousness and habit in our speech place us in positions of endless apology and regrets. Awareness and loving kindness in our speech generates simplicity.

What is it we refrain from? Words of cruelty and harshness that lead to pain. Sentiments that are truthful, yet spoken at a time or in a way that they cannot be recognized. Words that are used simply to fill uncomfortable silences. Words that are used as weapons to relieve us of the inner discomfort of anger and bitterness. Restraint is not just explored in the words that we speak to others, but in the way we speak to ourselves. The endless monologues of self-judgment, inner censorship, and criticism that that we inflict upon ourselves in our inner conversations can only lead to an increase in self-denial and a sense of worthlessness. Restraint in our speech is not about gagging or silencing ourselves, but about fostering simplicity and loving kindness.

Living a life of integrity, we commit ourselves to truthfulness, kindness, and simplicity in our speech. We appreciate the difference between simply making noise and letting our speech be a vehicle that communicates wisdom, healing, and loving kindness. A few words born of genuine concern and compassion mean more than volumes of prescriptive advice. In the days following the deaths of many young children in a small village, the pastor was asked to provide explanations and solutions by people needing to understand what had occurred. He asked everyone for silence, to create the space for listening, compassion, and empathy. In wise speech we learn to listen to the voices of our inner intentions before we speak, thus finding ourselves more able to listen to others. Learning to appreciate a greater silence within ourselves, our speech begins to communicate calmness and clarity.

Keeping a Clear Mind

We refrain from taking intoxicants that cloud the mind, committing ourselves instead to nurturing a mind that is clear and awake. A spiritual path is a path of waking up in our lives and of connecting with the simple truths of each moment. The addictions to drugs and alcohol lead us increasingly into the realms of disconnection, fantasy, and carelessness. It is not in times of great happiness, peace, or joy that we reach to such intoxicants, but mostly in times of pain, loneliness, confusion, or hurt. Experiences we want to escape or avoid. Intoxicants may provide a pseudo-happiness or sense of well-being, but it is a state of forgetfulness and is not sustainable. Emerging from the high of intoxication, the challenge of finding true happiness and freedom within ourselves feels even more insurmountable.

Freud once said that neurosis is the refusal to suffer. This does not imply a fatalistic acceptance of a daily diet of suffering, but it does suggest that to be free we need to be willing to embrace the experiences of discontent, alienation, and pain that come with living. Through learning to find peace and balance within them, rather than avoiding, suppressing, or denying them, we will find an unshakeable freedom. There is no spiritual path which is ethically neutral. A path of awakening is directed toward peace, openheartedness, compassion, and freedom. To treasure awakening is to treasure the end of sorrow and alienation in all its forms, to bring an end to the causes of sorrow. This is neither a narcissistic path concerned only with ending personal suffering, nor an abstract journey intent on achieving a liberation separate from the grist of our daily lives and relationships. A commitment to integrity enables us to be taught by the ordinary moments in our lives and to approach them with reverence.

Being awake to life means embracing the reality that moral certainties are often elusive. Definitive moments of right and wrong are superseded by many more moments where we simply do not know. Moral certainty is possessed by those who have not looked deeply into the countless ambiguities of human life. When we walk on the grass, countless creatures may die beneath our feet. How would we advise a friend in agony with terminal cancer if she begins to explore the possibility of ending her life? We give a pair of shoes to someone unable to afford them—and then notice that they have been manufactured in an Asian sweatshop. An anguished young woman, pregnant with the child of a rapist, asks us to support her in a termination. We do not always have the right answer but we accept that life asks of us a quality of compassion and understanding that is beyond the realm of right and wrong. A life of integrity asks us to forsake the false security of right and wrong. With empathy we go beyond the boundaries of opinion and judgment, and sense what it might mean to live within the heart and life of the person before us. In those moments we must ask ourselves, "What are the words, actions, and choices that are healing?" We cannot always guarantee the results of our choices, but we can learn to be clear in our intentions.

The Wisdom of Integrity

Integrity is the foundation for deepening wisdom, and it is the natural expression of an awakened heart. An enlightened mind is deeply immersed in an understanding of interdependence and it recognizes the transparency of the divisions created between "self" and "other." This is a natural and spontaneous integrity born of understanding the illusory nature of separation and disconnection. Milarepa, a great master, said, "Long accustomed to contemplating compassion, I no longer see a difference between myself and other." In deeply understanding the emptiness of the barriers created by a belief in "I" and "mine," reaching out to ease sorrow or pain is as natural as reaching in to ease the pain in one's own body. Inwardly liberated from greed, hatred, and delusion, the awakened mind finds a genuine home in honesty, respect, and compassion. Our body is no other than the bodies we see before us in different forms, sharing the same capacity to experience both pain and well-being. The heart and mind we encounter in another is essentially no other than our own heart and mind, with its capacity both for distress and for peace. Exploring the causes of sorrow, pain, and fear inwardly, we are essentially exploring *all* minds and hearts. The causes of the happiness, freedom, and joy we sense as possible within ourselves are shared with all living beings. There is no thing and no one in this world that is separate, independent, or disconnected. All life is woven in an eternal dance of interdependence. Understanding this deeply frees us to move beyond the boundaries of self-centeredness and be guided by compassion, kinship, and honesty; forsaking the habits of self-protection, greed, and anger. Peace and fearlessness are the taste of wise integrity.

> Better than a thousand careless words is one single word
> that gives peace.
> Better than a hundred years lived in heedlessness,
> Without contemplation,
> Is one single day lived in wisdom and deep contemplation.
> Better than a hundred years lives in confusion,
> Is a single day lived with courage and wise intention.
> THE DHAMMAPADA

GUIDED MEDITATION

Take a moment to reflect on relationships or times with others where there has been a tangible sense of trust, loving kindness, and safety. Sense the ways in which those relationships are treasured and allow you to deepen, open up, and be fearless. Be aware of the feelings of peace, well-being, and freedom that are embedded in those connections.

Take a moment to reflect on relationships that may be scarred by mistrust, judgment, or alienation. Sense the fear or unease that may arise in your body, the agitation that may appear in your heart and mind. What would be needed to heal those divisions? What intentions would need to be nurtured for the disconnection to be eased? Is it possible for you to find the loving kindness of body, heart, and mind to bring to an end the separation? Is it important for you?

CHAPTER

4

the mind

Nothing can do us more harm than a thought unguarded.
But once understood there is nothing that can be a greater friend,
not even your father or mother.

THE BUDDHA

In a life committed to integrity, the mind comes to rest with greater ease in calmness and simplicity. The mind that is at peace with itself finds peace in the world. In a heart of loving kindness there is a falling away of layers of confusion born of hatred, dishonesty, and greed. We can lay down the burden of all the residues and traces born of a disconnection with the world; we learn to release guilt, regret, fear, and self-consciousness. The calm mind is an accessible mind; we can explore its pathways, and mazes; we can understand it and find freedom within it.

If we are to find simplicity in our lives we need to find it within our own mind. If we are to find calm and peace in our lives, it will first be discovered within our mind. Learning to understand the nature of our mind, we find the sources of simplicity. Our mind can feel chaotic, unruly, overburdened, and unpredictable, seeming to have a life of its own independent of our aspirations and wishes. We try to tame it, subdue it, ignore it, and deny it; we need to learn to understand and befriend it. A keen gardener, intent on creating a perfect lawn, struggled desperately with the dandelions that just wouldn't go away. He read every manual, consulted experts, used every available weed killer to no avail. Each morning a new dandelion would appear. Finally, in despair, he consulted his neighbor, who had a perfect lawn. "Nothing works," he complained. "All my work is worthless, destroyed by these dandelions. Is there no solution?" The neighbor paused and answered, "I suggest you learn to love them." Our mind is no obstacle in our search for calm simplicity; it is no barrier to wisdom and peace; it can be embraced in the light of liberating, calm attention and become an ally.

The Power of Thought

Each moment, our personal world is born with our thoughts. Accompanying us through our days and nights, the lifelong companion of our mind creates and shapes the world we live in and the degree of happiness and sorrow we experience. Through our minds we can think our way into success or failure, tragedy or elation. With our thoughts we ascend to dizzying heights of pleasure through the fantasies, romantic dreams, and plans we weave. Just as quickly we can plunge into depths of despair as our mind takes us into the darkness of obsession, anxiety, and confusion. In our thoughts we meet the inner terrorist with its burden of judgment and blame, the endless replaying of the past and the rehearsals of the future. Equally, we meet the mind as an ally with its capacity for creativity, reflection, and investigation, and its power to communicate compassion, reconciliation, and wisdom. The Buddha once said, "Who is your enemy? The mind is your enemy. Who is your friend? The mind is your friend." The mind has been the source of destruction, war, and conflict in our world as well as the source of great healing, reconciliation, and creativity.

The average person is said to have more than 67 thousand thoughts each day, and in this waterfall of thinking we can gasp for ease and simplicity. The entrancing power of our thoughts takes us into the realms of heaven and hell as we lose ourselves in their webs of complexity. Our thoughts are embodied and made visible in our words, actions, and choices.

As Marcus Aurelius put it: "The universe is change: our life is what our thoughts make it." The sights, sensations, sounds, and events universal to all of us are weighed, and evaluated, laden with memory, likes and dislikes. What comforts one person terrorizes another; the event we may view as a disaster may be the greatest teacher to another. A man living on the border of China cherished his stallion above all else in his life. One day his horse escaped and was captured by the nomads across the border. Everyone tried to console him, but his father only said, "What makes you so sure this isn't a blessing?" Some months later his stallion returned home bringing with him a mate. The man was overjoyed at his good fortune, but his father only said, "What makes you so sure this isn't a disaster?" Riding his new horse one day he fell and broke his hip and was once more lost in despair. His father asked, "What makes you so sure this isn't a blessing?" Soon after, the nomads invaded the village and forced every able-bodied man into their army. The father and his lame son were spared this fate. Caught in the tangle of our preferences and judgments, friends and enemies, there is little ease to be found in the world. We will find simplicity in our lives only when we find it within our own minds. Just as the mind is the forerunner of confusion and complexity, it is also the forerunner of ease and well-being.

The Pathways of the Mind

To find simplicity in this tangled mental world we need to understand the mind and its pathways. As we give closer attention to the mind, we begin to see it as a tapestry of many colors. The mind is not just an uninterrupted, constant entity chattering its way through our lives, but a fluid process endlessly changing its shape and hue, arising and passing in different forms. The tapestry of our mind is formed on a moment-to-moment level by the feelings that arise, the perceptions we receive, the intentions that are formed; by what we pay attention to, and our responses to all of these. If we dwell in anger, anger grows; if we dwell in resentment our resentment becomes more and more solid with time; if we pay attention to compassion it, too, will grow; if we give attention to generosity our trust in it will deepen. Our inner world is shaped by what we give attention to, because this is where we make our home.

In Buddhist teaching the mind is a sense door that arises and passes just as do all the other sense doors. The gateway of seeing arises with a sight, hearing arises with a sound, body consciousness arises with sensation, smelling with a smell, tasting with a flavor. So too the mind arises and passes with its thoughts, perceptions, intentions, and feelings—planning, remembering, imagining, and dreaming; a constantly changing process. The capacity to see the mind as a sense door, a fluid process is a great relief, offering the possibility of simplicity and understanding. The Buddha once described this saying, "In the seeing, there is just the seeing; in the hearing there is just the hearing; in the thinking, there is just the thinking." Calm simplicity in the world of our mind is discovered through the wisdom of being able to strip away the excess layers of association, story, and comparison with which we surround the simplest perception.

When lost in the web of our thinking we rarely see the simplicity of our mind's pathways and movements. We catch sight of a person who has annoyed us in the past and our minds flood with our memories of that encounter with all its associated regrets, disappointments, and faded images of happiness. We catch a glimpse of someone who has previously delighted us and we experience a different flood of hopes, dreams, and ambitions with all their associated anxieties and excitements. Our preoccupations, aversions, and expectations, our fears, wants, and obsessions tangle us in webs of complexity. The mind loves to travel in familiar territory, endlessly recycling thoughts and images we have thought a thousand times before. We move through the world making it familiar through our concepts and labels. Walking through the garden, the world does not invite or command us to impose our thoughts of "good," "bad," "beautiful," and "ugly", yet we find ourselves freezing the universe into something known through concept, memory, and association. Within all this activity there is little room for surprise. Intuitively we may understand that our capacity to deepen and learn is linked to our capacity to be surprised—to be surprised by life, by other people, and by ourselves. Our concepts, ideas, and knowledge can only tell us what we think about the world, drawing on memory and association. To know anything fully we must learn to be still, to listen, and allow it to reveal itself to us.

We ride the roller coaster of highs and lows, interest and boredom, excitement and despair countless times a day. Exhausted and distracted by inner turbulence, the mind comes to be regarded as a problem, an obstacle, something to be avoided or overcome. We may align ourselves with an "anti-thought" philosophy, intent on eradicating our mind, believing we would be happy and calm if we had a different mind. Beginning to discover simplicity and ease within the mind starts with the willingness to step back a little and question, "Is the mind truly the problem? Does any single thought, memory, or image hold the intrinsic power to cause sorrow and despair?" The storms of the mind that shatter us may not be born of the arising and passing of thought, memory, or images, but of the climate of confusion and complexity that surrounds them.

The Power of the Mind

The mind is viewed as a problem because of its apparent power to cause excruciating sorrow, confusion, and fear. The unpredictability of the mind leaves us feeling we have no inner refuge of calm and balance. Enjoying a moment of calm and happiness, we are suddenly ambushed by a storm of negativity. Obsessions and resentments appear without warning; a simple encounter with another person turns into an elaborate story that swallows us. Driving to work and caught in traffic, the driver behind us suddenly honks his horn. Immediately the stories begin: "What am I doing wrong? Why is that person so aggressive? Am I going to be the latest victim of road rage?" As we drive off we look in our mirror and see the driver making a gesture of apology. He sounded his horn by mistake. These storms and dramas can end as quickly as they appeared, leaving us bewildered and exhausted. Our thoughts, memories, and images can lock us into closed rooms of resentment, fear, or shame where we feel powerless, the location of the key unknown. The unpredictable surges of our minds leave us fearful and insecure.

Apart from its unpredictability, the utterly convincing nature of the mind's constructions and dramas sentence us to inhabit inner worlds uniquely our own, yet we find ourselves certain of their absolute reality. A twinge in our knee, and in our thoughts we are already entering the operating theatre. A shared moment of happiness with another person, and within our thoughts we are arranging our marriage, celebrating the birth of our children, and dealing with the trauma of our divorce. Caught in the morning rush hour we spend our waiting moments weaving together each unfortunate event in our lives, convincing ourselves of our unworthiness and failure. We entertain both delightful and deeply painful stories, about ourselves, about others, and the nature of the world; yet our stories prevent us from seeing what is true in each moment. It is in seeing and connecting with the clear actuality of each moment, each encounter, each thought, that we discover simplicity and ease.

The uncontrollable, seemingly choiceless nature of our thoughts leads us to inhabit realms of obsession, anxiety, and fantasy far from where we wish to be. Rarely do we wake in the morning and decide this is a good day to be depressed, to be lost in fantasy, to reinforce resentment. Yet on a daily basis we commit countless moments of psychic vandalism as we live through our thought-created world. We feel out of control, governed by thoughts that lead to speech, actions and choices that feel unintentional, giving birth to a world removed from calm and simplicity. We resolve to be more generous and patient, only to find words of frustration flying from our mouths. We want to be more compassionate and feel appalled at the reappearance of the same old judgmental thoughts. The habits of the mind are powerful; wisdom teaches us we are not helpless.

In *The Dhammapada* the Buddha speaks of the power of our mind:

We are what we think,
All that we are arises with our thoughts.
With our thoughts we make the world.
Speak or act with an impure mind
And trouble will follow you
As the wheel follows the ox that draws the cart.
We are what we think.
All that we are arises with our thoughts.
With our thoughts we make the world.
Speak or act with a pure mind
And happiness will follow you
As your shadow, unshakable.
How can a troubled mind
Understand the way.

The Potential of the Mind

The mind has the potential to be a source of great sorrow and confusion, but it also holds the potential to be the mother of great simplicity and wisdom. The place where we discover serenity, insight, balance, depth, and vibrancy is not separate from the place where confusion, complexity, and agitation are generated. The great Zen master Dogen said, "In your meditation, you yourself are the mirror reflecting the solution of your problems. The human mind has absolute freedom within its true nature. You can attain this freedom intuitively. Don't work towards freedom but allow the work itself to be freedom."[1] In countless texts and in the experience of countless people, the mind is described as luminous, vibrant, radiant, and still. The mind which is limitless, shining, and transparent is the mind we are invited to discover in our quest for simplicity.

In learning to discover the mind of simplicity, the Buddha used the analogy of a magic show. A famous magician arrives in town and you join the crowd scrambling for seats. In speechless amazement you watch the miracles of people disappearing, rabbits appearing from nowhere, bodies cut in half, and other breathtaking illusions. Glancing around, you see that you share in the enchantment of the audience, believing in the reality of what is being created before your eyes. The mixture of drama and comedy is enjoyable when you know that what you are seeing is illusion. To believe those illusions to be real would be less enjoyable. Wanting to repeat the experience of intensity and elation, you return the following evening but this time find a quiet corner in the wings of the stage. Here the view is very different; you see the concealed wires and trapdoors hidden by the frenzied waving of the magic wand. The tricks no longer surprise you and the illusions no longer deceive. It is a show in which you are no longer a participant—you appreciate and applaud the artistry but you are awake.

1 *The Enlightened Mind*, Stephen Mitchell (ed), page 100.

We too can discover the transparency of our own magic show, to awaken from the stories and dreams, and rest in the calm simplicity born of seeing clearly the truths of each moment. What a marvelous world it would be if we could choose to have only pleasant thoughts, heartwarming memories, and delightful images. Reality tells us this will never be possible. Our experience tells us that our entrancement with the intensity, excitement, and drama of our enchanting stories will be matched by the sorrow that comes as we lose ourselves in disturbing, painful, and agitated stories. It is not the mind that causes pain, but our captivation in which simplicity is surrendered.

If you were to drop a jewel into a muddy pond, you would be unlikely to find it by taking a stick and frantically stirring it around. All you would achieve would be to make the water cloudy. To find your jewel it would be more effective to allow the water to settle, to look closely and carefully explore the pond systematically. The same patience and careful attention are called for to discover simplicity within our minds. We will not think ourselves out of complexity; it is not always possible for us to think our way into peace, calmness, or the liberating insights we seek. As Yogi Berra, the great baseball player, put it, "How can you think and hit at the same time?" Stillness, interest, curiosity, and sensitive attention will always be the pathways of simplicity.

Papanca—Thought Proliferation

In the Buddhist tradition there is a gem of a word, *papanca*, which illustrates the ways in which we weave our stories and move from simplicity to complexity, from a universal world to a personal one on a moment-to-moment level. *Papanca* defines the multiplicity and proliferation of thought that distorts and colors the way things actually are in each moment. Depending upon the thoughts we think, the stories we construct about the world assume a particular color and meaning that is unique and personal to us; the world becomes a magic show. The origin of all our stories begins in the simple contact of the sense gate with the sense information. A friend invites you out for dinner and the moment you walk into the restaurant you notice a particular odor and you recognize it— garlic. This initial impression may be followed by a flood of thoughts and associations. You may have pleasant memories of the last time you fell in love in an Italian restaurant, remembering how the romance unfolded and ended; you begin salivating in anticipation not only of a wonderful meal, but also the possibility of a new romance. It could happen that you have unpleasant feelings and associations with the smell of garlic. You remember the indigestion, resent your companion for inviting you to such an unsuitable place, resent your body for imposing so many restrictions upon you. The magic show begins and you are lost.

Sometimes we emerge from these mind storms with a retrospective wisdom that understands that we did not need to enter into such agitation, yet even this awareness can be frustrating as time and time again we fall for the magic of the mind. The creation of our magic shows is rooted in our likes and dislikes, the opinions and beliefs we hold, and the entire range of ideas, images, and identities we hold to be true about ourselves. The Buddha once said, "One who does not grasp hold of anything is not agitated. One who is not agitated is close to freedom."

The basic ingredients of the stories we weave are simple—the sense doors: our eyes, ears, tongue, nose, body, and mind. Received by the sense door is the sense information—sights, sounds, tastes, smells, sensations and thoughts, images, and memories. Through perception we recognize the world and into those bare perceptions we weave the ingredients of unwise attention, expectation and resistance, likes and dislikes, super-imposed association, and the creation of our personal inter-pretation of the moment. It is within this process of entrancement that we can also find illuminating simplicity and wisdom. A path of awakening would never suggest that we should be a passive and unwitting spectator of our own repeated disasters, but should turn the power of our attention to untangle the web of complexity.

A certain meditation center in America is a magnet for all the local dogs who know that whenever they appear they will be showered with affection and attention. Every day, of course, there are moments when their love of attention competes with the compelling needs of their stomachs, which tell them to go home to be fed. Following the dictates of its stomach, one of the dogs will begin its homeward journey only to be distracted by a passing walker who offers a kind word or caress which makes the dog turn around and follow them, wanting more. Intention sabotaged by a new compelling sensation; over and over again the dog is caught in this tension. It can take a long time for it to make its way home. We find ourselves caught in a similar tension, longing for calm, stillness, and simplicity, yet through habit and confusion following pathways of entanglement and complexity.

Wise and Unwise Attention

What is unwise attention? Grasping at the sensory information we receive, and weaving into that initial grasping our memories, fears, expectations, likes and dislikes, thus creating a mind and world of complexity. What is wise attention? Being wholeheartedly present within the same sensory information, aware of the associations that may arise and yet grasping nowhere—discovering a mind that is immeasurable and boundless. We can learn to cultivate wise attention by learning to listen to our own minds. A sight is received fully and let go of; a sound listened to wholeheartedly and released; thoughts appear, are known deeply, and allowed to pass.

The appearance of thoughts in our minds holds no intrinsic power to cause sorrow or complexity. It may be remarkable that we can experience so many thoughts; what is even more remarkable is that we invest them with the authority to determine our well-being and happiness. A thought of anger arises in us and we determine ourselves to be an "aggressive" person. It is replaced a moment later with an affectionate thought and our sense of identity undergoes another transformation. The changing identities we experience in a single day are determined by our thoughts. In truth, they are just thoughts that can be received in a spacious, sensitive awareness. We can all learn to listen more closely to our thoughts, learn from them and discover what it means not to be confined by them.

Finding space and simplicity within the mind is born of our willingness to listen to our own thoughts and to trace their pathways and movements to their source. We can make moments in our day when we consciously listen to the waterfall of our thinking, rather than just habitually thinking. What do we discover when we intentionally turn our attention to examine and investigate the movements of our minds? The babble of many voices clamors for space within the mind. The voices of planning, hoping, worrying, chattering, controlling, liking and disliking, and ordering, capture our attention, leaving the mind feeling constricted and narrow. We hear the voices of judgment, fear, expectation, fantasy, and regret. As we listen more closely we begin to notice that all these voices and thoughts arise and pass, appear and disappear, like all other sounds, sights, and sensations.

Consciously select just one of the thoughts that appear and hold it in your attention: "I want happiness" or "I need love," and notice what happens in your mind. A gateway to many other thoughts may be opened, but continue to explore what happens as you bring your attention back to your initial thought. The mind begins to soften and open around it. We discover that we cannot intentionally think habitually; habit in every area of our life requires inattention. The thought "I want happiness" will not linger when it is no longer supported by expectation, aversion, fear, or grasping. It will appear and it will disappear. We are learning to let go, to let all things be. Our thoughts are liberated from their burdens of association and habit; they no longer hold the authority to determine our well-being or our sorrow.

The Vastness of Mind

If we take some moments to look at the sky, we see the way our attention is drawn to what appears in the sky—the clouds, the sun, the rainbows, the showers. If we focus only on what appears, we notice the way in which our mind becomes constricted by our preference, like and dislikes, our ideas of how things "should be," to the extent that we no longer notice the vastness of the sky. It is this vastness that holds all that appears in it without preference, equally embracing the darkness of the clouds and the brightness of the sun. Intrinsically, the mind rests in the same vastness with its capacity to hold thoughts of love, care, and happiness as well as thoughts of anxiety, negativity, or control. It would be a futile effort to endeavor constantly to rearrange and reorder our mental world so we had only the pleasant, flattering, and supportive thoughts. It would be a wiser effort to discover the vast spaciousness of the mind that embraces all yet dwells nowhere.

Dwelling and constriction are not the fault of the mind; it is without blame; they are born of habit, inattention, and fear.

Learning to see the arising and passing, the impermanence of all thoughts, we discover a greater ease within them; we learn to withdraw authority from the contents of our thoughts and discover the liberating authority of our capacity to see clearly. As long as we live our mind will have thoughts just as our body will have sensations. Withdrawing our expectations and fears, our likes and dislikes, none of these thoughts are enemies. Discovering space within our mind we learn to befriend all thoughts without exception. There is the story of a man shot by an arrow. His friends run to help but, as they reach out to draw the arrow out of his arm, the wounded man stops them, saying "Hold on a minute. Before you touch that arrow I want to know what direction it came from, what kind of wood it's made from and who the archer was." As thoughts arise we are not always obliged to follow them, to ascertain where they came from or be lost in them. We can learn to let them be and they will pass; we can learn to find calm simplicity and stillness everywhere.

In the search for simplicity we can learn to explore the space between thoughts. Listening closely to our mind, the thoughts begin to slow down. We discover that just as the out-breath is followed by a pause before the in-breath, there is also space between the thoughts. We learn to seek the gaps—the space between sounds, between sensations, between thoughts, and to explore the nature of these gaps. The gaps are the home of the mind, the limitless silence of the mind. Thoughts arise in that silence and fall back into silence. Exploring the nature of silence we begin to understand that it is not dependent on the absence of thought but is the prevailing sound that permeates all thought. Silence is profoundly simple—resisting nothing, wanting nothing, lacking in nothing yet present and complete in all moments.

GUIDED MEDITATION

Learning to befriend our mind we discover its creative capacity to reflect, understand, and illuminate. Creativity and simplicity are closely bonded. Rarely do we find any creative gesture, word, or movement that is born of a mind that is agitated, compulsive, or constricted. The greatest moments of creativity in our lives are born of our capacity to listen and be still. Reflection is an inner exploration, a way of nurturing intuition and wisdom.

Take some moments in your day when your mind is calm and consciously invite into those spaces a simple question:

- "What is happiness?"
- "What more do I need in this moment to be free?"
- "What is peace?"

In those times of calmness, invite into your mind a pattern of thinking or obsessing that has been haunting you and again pose one or two simple questions:

- "What do I need to let go of to be at peace with this person, this event, this memory?"
- "Why am I holding on?"

Listen inwardly to the responses that rise up to surround these questions. Let go of the demand for answers or the need for resolution and consciously stay with the questions. Treasure no conclusions or opinions.

If the mind becomes agitated or begins to travel well-worn pathways, let go of the question and take your attention to listening to sounds and the space between sounds until calmness returns. Return once more to the question and listen inwardly. Wise thought, the capacity for reflection and investigation, is one of the powerful keys that awakens insight.

Listening to the mind we discover space and silence. When the mind rests in spaciousness we finds spaciousness in all corners of our lives. When the mind rests in simplicity, we discover simplicity in all things. Our mind and heart are one. A clear mind, rooted in simplicity and integrity, no longer battles with the world. We discover the heart of compassion.

compassion

Accustomed long to contemplating Love and Compassion
I have forgotten all difference
Between myself and others.

MILAREPA

COMPASSION springs from a mind and heart deeply rooted in simplicity, integrity, and a profound understanding of the interconnected nature of all life. Compassion is a transforming quality of heart we cultivate, nurture, and refine. It is redis-covered through the falling away of the layers of fear, resistance, and anxiety that have the power to veil the innately compassionate heart. Our challenge may not be so much one of becoming more compassionate, but one of learning to let go of the clouds of confusion that obscure the powerful compassion within us.

There is no greater need in this world than the need for compassion. There is no greater healing power than that of compassion. Nurturing compassion invites us to address the most challenging questions and dilemmas of our times. How do we respond to the escalating poverty, suffering, and anguish in the world? Can we find a wise and compassionate way to embrace those who abuse, exploit, and oppress? Can we find a way to embrace the rage, fear, and hurt carried in our own hearts? Is there any true alternative to compassion? Compassion is a seed, cultivated within ourselves, that flowers in kindness, patience, tolerance and the skillful responses of healing. Compassion is born not of complex, heroic efforts and prescriptions, but of a simple dedication to the end of sorrow as it is met in each moment.

Recently the Dalai Lama met with a friend, an elderly Tibetan monk who had fled from Tibet to rejoin the Tibetan community in exile after spending twenty years in Chinese prisons and labor camps; two decades in which he had faced unimaginable brutality, isolation, and fear. The Dalai Lama asked him, "Were there ever times when your life was truly in danger?" The monk paused, then answered, "There were only a few occasions when I faced real danger, and those were the occasions I was in danger of losing my compassion for the Chinese."

In reading his words, listen deeply to the responses that arise within you. We may feel humbled by such immense courage, inspired and grateful that there continue to be people in this world who embody remarkable love and compassion in the midst of great adversity. We may be tempted to idealize and deify the monk who spoke them, believing him to possess, through years of arduous meditation, spiritual powers and qualities not available to us. We need to remember that compassion is not only the territory of the saintly, the realized, or the religious; it is born of heartfelt listening to our own life, heart, and mind, and hearing the echoes of all lives, hearts and minds.

Sorrow, pain, and confusion are not only experienced by the foolish, the misguided, or the cruel. Loss, fear, division, and anger are universal illnesses, felt by us all, and they are healed by understanding and the power of compassion. Each of us has the capacity to awaken our own hearts and minds, and discover the simplicity of genuine compassion. The Buddha was once asked, "Would it be true to say that part of our meditation practice is for the development of love and compassion?" He answered, "It would not be true to say this; it would be true to say that the whole of our meditation practice is for the development of love and compassion."

We can translate the words of the Tibetan monk into our own lives and explore our responses to them: "The times of greatest danger in our lives are the occasions we are in danger of losing our own home in a compassionate heart." There are moments in life when we have little compassion for ourselves, painful moments when the embracing of inner sorrow and pain with compassion is replaced by harsh inner voices of guilt, judgment, shame, and blame. There are moments when our heartfelt listening to the suffering and pain of other people turns to indifference, prescriptive advice, or blame. We encounter painful moments in our relationships with people who have harmed or threatened us, when our intrinsic connectedness is submerged beneath a complexity of fear, anger, and resentment. In this loss of compassion we are terrorized by inner forces of alienation and division that undermine our well-being, imprisoning us in separation and fear.

Separation and Interconnectedness

Compassion is essentially simple. We share with all life the capacity for feeling, the experience of having a body, mind, and heart in continual interface with countless other bodies, minds, and hearts. Our capacity to feel deeply means we share with all life the possibility of experiencing delight, joy, trust, and intimacy, just as we share in the capacity to experience pain, sorrow, grief, and fear. Living within a physical body, we all share the experience of aging, frailty, illness, and death, just as we share the precious times of strength, health, safety, and vitality. Through our minds we share the capacity to experience confusion, agitation, and complexity, just as we share the possibilities of serenity, clarity, and balance. An understanding of this profound interconnectedness of all life is at the root of the compassionate heart dedicated to alleviating suffering without reservation or exception.

What happens when we lose touch with our capacity for compassion? In the loss of compassion, a gulf of separation emerges, an apparently unbridgeable gap between "self" and "other," "I" and "you," "us" and "them." This is not an empty divide—the gulf of separation holds an ocean of feeling. In the loss of compassion this gulf fills with feelings of anger, blame, fear, hatred, and resentment; painful feelings that serve to widen and solidify the division.

In the loss of our heartfelt capacity to receive and embrace sorrow and distress, we lose one of the most precious and liberating gifts it is possible for us to know. We lose our understanding of interconnectedness and in doing so we lose the most true, authentic core of our being. Cast adrift from an understanding of interconnectedness, we become captives of the complexity of fear, anger, blame, and isolation. This is the greatest of all suffering.

We can find ourselves feasting on a daily diet of isolation and separation. Take a moment to reflect on a person from your past or present whom you struggle with, who may have harmed or hurt you with words of rejection, with abuse or blame, and notice the feelings and responses that emerge. Perhaps you can sense a slight hardening of the heart, feelings of resistance or tension, or a flood of memories, past conversations, and events. Connecting with that person even from a distance may open the door to such powerful feelings of agitation, fear, or anger that we instinctively flee from them into fantasies or daydreams.

We are strangely close to the people in our lives we struggle with, fear, or resent, just as we are close to the difficult places in our own hearts and minds—our tendencies towards self-abasement, greed, or feelings of inadequacy. These difficult places and relationships occupy a pivotal role in our lives and hearts. We think about them endlessly; we obsess far more about the difficult people in our lives, analyzing their imperfections, replaying the historical and familiar story of resentment, than we think about the people we love and enjoy. Endless time is spent dwelling upon, judging, and analyzing our own imper- fections, the many ways in which we disappoint ourselves. How much time do we give to appreciating and celebrating our own tenderness, generosity, and sensitivity? Tremendous energy is consumed in planning our strategies of avoidance, modifying or eliminating the relationships we struggle with, endeavoring to perfect ourselves by rejecting everything we deem imperfect. In all of these endeavors we tend the garden of separation and sorrow. Who are the real enemies in our lives? Mostly they are the people who we are no longer willing to listen to and the places in ourselves we deny.

The difficult people in our lives, the difficult places in ourselves, appear to hold so much power, but it is a power we have given to them. As we become captivated by the complexity of resentment, anxiety, and judgment, we delegate the authority to define our well-being, happiness, and freedom to the difficult person or part of ourselves. We also believe that once we have removed the difficult person from our lives or once we have improved and perfected ourselves we will be happy, compassionate, and free, not understanding the futility and painfulness of this quest. Ram Dass once put it, "I'd rather be happy, than right." We could ask ourselves, "Would we rather flounder in the waves of resentment or find the compassion to forgive and move on in our lives? Would we rather pursue the desperate dream of perfection or find the wisdom and compassion of acceptance and understanding?"

In the loss of compassion, and the surrender of the core of freedom within, there is real grieving in our hearts; the grief of profound loss. Learning to rediscover our capacity for compassion is a reclaiming of authority. Reclaiming an understanding of interconnectedness, authority is found in what is true, in the simple truth that in separation and alienation there is suffering, pain, and limitation. In resting in interconnectedness there is peace, forgiveness, compassion, and vastness. The Sufi Rumi once said:

> Out beyond ideas of wrongdoing and rightdoing
> There is a field. I'll meet you there.
> When the soul lies down in that grass,
> The world is too full to talk about
> Ideas, language, even the phrase each other
> Doesn't make any sense

Our memories, thoughts, and fears that are rooted in pain speak the language of separation and division—"wrong," "bad," "unworthy." The wisdom of our heart speaks a softer language—"patience," "tolerance," "forgiveness." It is the language of the yearning to be free from suffering, to discover intimacy with all things.

Learning to Listen

In the Chinese Buddhist tradition compassion is expressed in the form of Kuan Yin—her arms and eyes are open, receptive, and connected. Translated, her name is "One who listens to the sounds of the universe." In the Tibetan tradition it is the deity Avalokiteshvara, with his thousand eyes to see suffering and his thousand arms to reach out to suffering, who embodies enlightened compassion. In Pali, the word Karuna translates as "the heart that trembles in response to suffering." In the English language, compassion is to feel with life, to feel with suffering; to rest in a heart of profound empathy undistorted by thought of separation. The Buddha was once asked what compassion is and he answered, "If you want to know what compassion is, look into the eyes of a mother as she cradles her fevered, ill child." Compassion is a true vastness of heart and a depth of wisdom that listens to, embraces, and receives suffering. It is an antidote to hostility, resistance, and division. Learning to listen to the sounds of the universe is learning to soften and melt our armory of fear, mistrust, and imprisonment in a separate self.

Compassion is not a quality to romanticize, idealize, or project into a future moment. Nurturing compassion does not depend upon personal perfection. We meet suffering, pain, and confusion every day of our lives. The homeless person on the street, the frail parent, the hurt child, the stressed executive, the alienated teenager. It is not easy to open our hearts to the bottomless depths of pain in the world. We hold in our hearts our own mortality and the mortality of others. All life is fragile; we live in a fragile world. Health turns to illness, well-being to pain, safety to uncertainty, life to death; none of us can control the countless supports upon which our well-being rests. The moments of sorrow and confusion we meet are moments that invite us to cultivate a listening heart, to let go of separation, and to be present with every cell of our being. The difficult moments and encounters in our lives are the gateways of compassion. Our enemies are angels of compassion in disguise, inviting us to be present, to attend, and to receive. Here we discover for ourselves the healing, balancing power of compassion.

In my early years of practice in India, my teacher spent months giving me instruction in nurturing compassion. Living high on the mountain side, young, healthy, and surrounded by good friends, it was not difficult to gaze down upon the plains of India and the countless people enduring poverty, deprivation, and illness, and feel an outpouring of compassion for their pain. I remember thinking at the time that this wasn't a difficult practice—really quite enjoyable. Once I needed to come down from the mountain to travel to New Delhi to take care of some business. As I got on the bus, the conductor chose that moment to begin berating a poor, elderly villager who hadn't the money to pay for his ticket, shouting at him and attempting to force him off the bus. Within moments I found myself shouting in an equally aggressive voice at the conductor, berating and condemning him. Perhaps it would have been an appropriate response if it had been undertaken with mindfulness and wisdom. In truth it was pure anger. This was a most powerful lesson in nurturing compassion, inviting me to explore what it would mean to say "No" in that moment without being lost in my own rage. Compassion was also needed to soften the judgmental thoughts that arose in me about my sense of failure and spiritual deficiency. Genuine compassion is not only a response to obvious sorrow and pain, but is also present in the moments we are confronted with people who offend, threaten, or challenge us. This entails not condoning or consenting to unacceptable words and actions that cause violation, oppression, or pain; while not departing from the wisdom and compassion that is able to forgive and understand.

We will all meet many difficult moments in our lives—people will abuse us or take us for granted, people we love will leave us; our expectations of others and ourselves will be disappointed, and there will be times when we are misunderstood or judged unfairly. The difficult encounters and moments in our lives spiral into complexity when aversion and fear are layered upon them. With aversion come innumerable ideas about how we think the world, other people, and ourselves should be, together with our strategies for turning those ideas into reality. With fear is born in our imagination what might befall us, the endless possibilities of misfortune, and our desire to flee from difficulties. Oscar Wilde once said, "The most terrible things in my life never actually happened." In case they do, we want to be well rehearsed.

There is a simpler way of being with the difficult and painful in this life; to listen closely, to stay present, to investigate, and question—"Here is suffering. There are causes that can be understood without blame. What is the path to the end of suffering in this moment?" The path may involve intervention, the courage to say "no," wise action; it may involve forgiveness, tolerance, or patience. Whether our response to suffering is an inner or an outer one, compassion roots itself in the dedication to ending sorrow. Our capacity to make peace with the difficult is hindered and made complex through the added ingredients of aversion, fear, and avoidance. These are the layers of complexity that we can learn to understand and release.

Responding to Pain

The Buddha was once asked, "What is the wise way of responding to suffering?" He answered by explaining the possible paths of response, some that would lead to complexity and increased suffering, and others that would lead to compassion and the end of suffering. He spoke of the path of despair and powerlessness that only leads to a darkness of heart. "Why is this happening to me? Life is unfair." He spoke of the path of blame and of the agitation and disconnection that follow in the wake of blame. "It is your fault, it is you who make me suffer." He spoke of the path of guilt, the exaggerated sense of responsibility that claims all suffering as personal failure. "It is my fault, my inadequacy that has brought this sorrow." He spoke too of the path of investigation, the compassionate exploration of sorrow and struggle; an exploration that is concerned not so much with denying suffering, as with understanding its cause and its end. It is an exploration that acknowledges that not all pain can be eradicated, but that there may be a way of discovering freedom within the painful, and the end of suffering. This is the path of compassionate simplicity.

Compassion is concerned with bringing to stillness the agitation and fear of our own hearts, bridging the gap of disconnection, separation, and distance. It does not mean that pain will always disappear or that we will discover a solution to every dispute and conflict. We cannot always fix every event of distress, but we can always be present, awake, and receive each moment with compassion and simplicity.

Faced with difficult, painful situations and people in our lives, our minds and hearts become ensnared in frenzied attempts to find a solution or explanation. In the efforts we make to alter, modify, and fix, we become caught up in a despair that leads us to avoidance or suppression. Our compassion, that leads us to reach out, to help, and heal, is hijacked by the desperate desire to make pain disappear. Too often we are left feeling frustrated and powerless. Some years ago, a gunman burst into a school and opened fire on a classroom of children. Amid the devastating grief and bewilderment that followed, a journalist asked the parish priest, "How do you explain what has happened here? You're a religious leader and many people feel that they need an explanation. How could this happen, how could someone do this?" The priest answered, "To try to explain this event is not the way. This is not the time for trying to understand something of this order." There is not always an answer or a satisfactory explanation for the pain in the world. Suffering is held most fully in a still, receptive, responsive silence. The words of healing, the responses of courage and wisdom, are born of that simplicity. Compassion is not just an accident, a random moment of openness. The still simplicity of the listening heart is always available to us; learning to let go gently of our demands for answers and resolutions, liberates the heart to listen.

Active Compassion

A heart without boundaries does not imply a surrender of discriminating wisdom—knowing what contributes and feeds suffering, and what brings it to an end. The simple receptivity of compassion may need to be translated into words, actions, and choices that ask for courage and wisdom. Inner stillness and simplicity is not only the birthplace of compassion, but also of wise action and response. Wise action is rarely born of fear, blame, or hatred, which only breed a further separation and division that perpetuates grief, loss, and pain. In a demonstration in Lhasa, the angry demonstrators came face to face with the equally angry soldiers. As the demonstration became increasingly frenzied, a terrified demonstrator found himself looking into the terrified eyes of a soldier who had dropped his gun. The young man picked up the gun, emptied it of its bullets, and handed it back to the soldier. How many moments in our lives do we face the choice between participating in the perpetuation of pain and finding another path that asks of us a greater courage, faith, and compassion?

Compassion is rooted in the simple understanding of inter-connectedness, the understanding of the transparency of separation. A Christian mystic once said, "Of what avail is the open eye if the heart is blind?" It could equally be said, "Of what avail is the open heart if the eye is blind?" Wisdom rescues compassion from deteriorating into feelings of pity and powerlessness. Compassion rescues wisdom from deteriorating into idealistic intentions that remain distant from the realities of suffering in each moment. The seeds of compassion and wisdom lie in each moment that we are willing to turn our attention toward suffering, pain, and conflict rather than following the pathways of denial or avoidance. The willingness to be present in the presence of suffering is the first step to softening the bands of aversion and fear that separate us from ourselves and others. In this shift of attention, we learn the primary lessons of listening and simplicity; we learn to ease the clamoring inner voices that demand formulas, solutions, and prescriptions. Learning to be wholeheartedly present, receptive in the midst of conflicts and divisions, we have the possibility of understanding not only the path to the end of suffering but also the causes of suffering.

The Faces of Pain

In the cultivation of compassion we intentionally bring attention to all the dimensions and moments of suffering per-ceivable to us. Embraced in our attention are the inexplicable, bewildering places and experiences of suffering that thwart all explanation. A child is devastated by illness, a loving person is wounded senselessly by another, a terrorized family is caught in someone else's war, people are unpredictably overtaken by circumstances that shatter every vestige of security. Such moments of suffering often stun us into helpless silence. In learning to listen to the universe we turn our attention to the fragile nature of all life experience—success turns to failure, pleasure to pain, joy to sorrow, gain to loss, the never ending story of life. The suffering that comes with ageing, illness, and death is invited into our awareness. Life is fragile, dependent upon so many factors beyond our control. Compassion rescues us from despair and blame, teaching us to be a steadfast presence in the storms of life, finding a refuge in compassionate listening.

We turn our attention to those places and relationships of suffering where there is a visible chain of events that lead to profound sorrow—the abuser, the rapist, the exploiter. Condoning, excusing, or justifying is not required of us, but wisdom *is*. Can we ever truly find the beginning of hatred, abusiveness, or rage in anyone? Where are the beginnings of our own anger, fear, judgment, or resentment? Their lineage goes back in time, generations before we were born. In our relationship with those people and moments where we are most easily inclined to condemn, we are asked to bring separation to an end, to withdraw blame and to soften the rage in our hearts; to bring a compassionate presence. We begin to understand that to listen wholeheartedly, we are asked to be empty —not absent, but empty of judgment, fear, resistance, and blame. These are the activities of separation and they are powerless to heal suffering or division. Compassion is never passive; the injustice, deprivation, and alienation in our world cries out for change and we are asked to respond. We need to act, to engage, and participate in that change. It is not always grand or heroic gestures that are called for, but a compassionate awareness of how we engage with the people and events in our life. How do we treat our neighbor, the drug addict on the street, our family, the annoying colleague? Are there ways we can be present in these encounters where we are not bound by habitual fear or aversion? Can we learn to listen more closely and find the words, actions, and care to touch the heart of another?

The gentle exploration of pain and sorrow in the world around us is also an exploration of the pain and sorrow we encounter in our own hearts and lives. Misfortune is part of our lives—events and circumstances unfold in unpredictable ways that introduce us to loss, uninvited sorrow, and disappointment, leaving in their wake feelings of helplessness and despair.

In the town where I live, one of the residents is a middle-aged homeless man who daily takes his place on the sidewalk. He used to have a job, a family, and a home. He also had a breakdown, became suicidal, and was hospitalized for a time. On his release he walked through his front door, saw the stack of bills and demands waiting for him, and walked out again to live on the street. His story could be the story of any one of us. We live in a fragile world and there is wisdom in embracing a wise insecurity, understanding that the only authentic refuge in this fragile life lies in our capacity to remain present, balanced, and compassionate. Endeavoring to secure and protect ourselves against fear and change is a heroic, yet futile effort. Compassion, the deep willingness to stand still and be receptive in the midst of pain, rescues us from blame and fear; it is simplicity embodied.

The conflict and struggle of greed, fear, and anger perceived in the world is reflected in the microcosm of the struggle and conflict in our own hearts. We encounter our own demons in the forces and patterns of relationships that cause pain to others and to ourselves. We speak words we regret, act in ways that harm others. We hold the power to wound ourselves with judgment, harshness, and blame, occupying the role of our own inner terrorist. All the strategies, formulas, and willpower in the world are no substitute for compassion. Rather than entangling ourselves in their complexity, we can take the time to be still and listen, to hold in compassionate attention the waves of regret, anger, guilt, and fear, without the additional layers of judgment. These moments of stillness are the deepest moments of learning in our lives. We begin to be able to trace suffering to its source and new pathways of response open up to us. A compassionate heart is not an idealized heart that never experiences anger, greed, or self-centeredness, but is the receptive presence that listens to those voices and receives them—without permitting them to be the guiding force of our actions, speech, and choices.

Doubt and Fear

The saboteurs of compassion are doubt and fear, born of a belief in self and separation. The allies of compassion are faith and courage, born of wisdom and commitment. We may doubt our capacity to endure pain, fearing we may be submerged or overwhelmed. We may doubt the power of compassion to heal, to transform ourselves and others. We may fear compassion will leave us weak, indecisive, or deprived of the capacity for skillful action. It is evident that suffering is the inevitable companion of separation and division, but we may fear losing separation believing that it protects us from vulnerability and pain. Mistrusting our own capacity for compassion, we may find ourselves seeking refuge in numbness. A teenage boy, in his third year of taking anti-depressants said, "If you care too much you get hurt. It's dangerous to care." Compassion teaches us that it is dangerous for our planet, our society, and ourselves *not* to care.

The great Tibetan yogi, Milarepa, went out one day to gather firewood. On his return he found his cave occupied by a tribe of fierce demons. Some were screeching, some were vandalizing his cave, others were performing magic tricks. Terrified, Milarepa drew on every strategy he had ever learned in his long history of meditation to rid his cave of the demons. He chanted mantras, tried to negotiate with them, invoked protection from the deities, prostrated himself before them. One by one the demons disappeared until only one remained, the fiercest of them all. Having exhausted all his formulas and strategies, Milarepa approached and placed his head in the mouth of the demon, whereupon the demon dissolved and turned into a rainbow.

Learning what it means to be empty and transparent is the daily path of the wise. It is a path that does not require a bulging portfolio of knowledge and technique, but the simple commitment on a moment-to-moment level to let go of the forces that obscure compassion. We learn to loosen our hold on resentment, demand, and fear. We learn to let go of our stories rooted in the past and our anxieties about the future. We learn to let go of our "shoulds," historical angers, and opinions. We learn to listen wholeheartedly in each moment and to understand suffering and its causes. A moment of letting go is a moment of listening to the universe in which all thoughts of "I" and "you" dissolve. Learning to let go of the heart of separation, the heart of compassion can emerge. Patient, kind, tolerant, and forgiving, compassion is the mother of calm simplicity.

GUIDED MEDITATION

Take a few moments to sit quietly, relax your body, and be still. Invite into your attention the sorrow and pain of someone you know who has been overtaken by misfortune—a friend who is sick, someone who is bereaved, someone who is struggling with feelings of rejection or hurt. Hold the image of that person in your heart and be aware of your responses—the sorrow, empathy, and compassion that arise. Silently offer to that person your heartfelt wishes for their healing.

■ "May you find peace. May you find healing."

Invite into your heart a person you struggle with or are alienated from, and be aware of the feelings and responses that emerge. What would happen if you were able to let go of the resentments and stories of the past? Can you see that person as yourself in another form? What would be needed for the healing of that separation? When the time is right, offer your heartfelt wishes for healing and forgiveness.

■ "For whatever words or actions I have expressed that have harmed you, I ask your forgiveness."
■ "I forgive you for the words and actions you have expressed that have harmed me."

Take a few moments to sense the places in your own heart where fear, anger, or harshness live, and offer to yourself your heartfelt wishes for healing and freedom.

■ "May I be at peace. May I find the trust and openness to befriend this anger, this fear, to soften this harshness."

Listening to the moment, to yourself, free of resistance or judgment, sense the stirring of compassion for yourself, for all beings.

6

emotion

The only lasting beauty is the beauty of the heart.

RUMI

ON the evening of the Buddha's enlightenment, the young prince Siddhartha sat beneath the Bodhi tree with an unshakeable resolve to be still and present until he was free. During the course of the night, Mara, the forces of delusion and con-fusion, assaulted him with every possible temptation in an attempt to divert him from his intention to awaken. Mara appeared in the disguise of delightful and pleasurable forms and promises, reminding Siddhartha of the countless sensual moments he was sacrificing. Mara manifested in the form of anger and hatred, inviting Siddhartha to follow the pathways of resentment and blame. Greed, lust, doubt, and fear all arose during the course of that night. Siddhartha's response was not one of resistance, agitation, denial, or fear, but to turn to face Mara and simply say "I know you." Those few words embodied Siddhartha's unwavering commitment to his journey and to his refusal to follow the pathways of confusion and complexity he had trodden a thousand times before. Unable to shake Siddhartha's unfaltering commitment to liberation, the poisonous arrows of Mara fell harmlessly to the ground.

The words "I know you" express more than just a superficial recognition of the powers of Mara, but embody the profound attitude of openness, welcome, and balance that lies at the heart of all paths of awakening. Nothing that touches us is unwelcome, everything we can feel and experience is worthy of our wholehearted attention. The archetypal story of Siddhartha's awakening is a story of vision, dedication, and freedom. It is a pilgrimage, a sacred journey of diving deeply into ourselves, where we meet our dragons and our angels. It is a story of faith, trusting that we hold within ourselves the possibility of discovering the same unshakability and freedom discovered by Siddhartha.

Imagine a different story, in which we hear the tale of a young man or woman who accidentally stumbled upon a Bodhi tree as they wandered in confusion through the forest; who then decided to stay for as long as it wasn't uncomfortable, the mosquitoes weren't troublesome, and their knees didn't ache. Perhaps they brought with them a picnic basket in case of hunger, their cherished blanket, and their mobile phone in case of boredom. They may have already decided that if any of these eventualities were to happen, they would give up, and return home to an easier life. It would look less like a pilgrimage than an accident that would require the rewriting of the entire Buddhist tradition.

Our own path of awakening will not be a replica of anyone else's. We all bring to this adventure our individual stories, histories, and sense of possibilities. Genuine freedom is never found through transcending our own stories, but in learning to find freedom within them. A path of awakening is a path of untangling, undoing the many layers of belief that blind us to the innate freedom within us. It is a journey that can hold moments of great joy as we discover the depth of stillness and peace possible for us, and moments of great pain as we discover the depths of fear and imprisonment in our beliefs. Above all, it is a path of honesty, where we ask to embrace everything in the light of calm acceptance. Speaking to a despairing student, the Buddha said, "If I did not have the faith that it was possible for you to walk this path, I would not ask it of you. Because I have total faith that it is possible for you to discover immeasurable freedom, I ask it of you."

We can hold images of an ideal spiritual path where we take our seat and plunge into depths of bliss, peace, calm, and compassion. For most people the experience of taking their seat upon a cushion is a direct encounter with every aspect of themselves, including the dragons they would rather ignore. It is difficult even to find a linear progression; moments of great calm are followed by moments of great agitation. Moments of peace and stillness, when we finally begin to assure ourselves of our progress, are overtaken by intense storms of doubt and unease. We are meeting the landscape of our hearts and it is here we are asked to discover unshakeable balance and freedom. Within the roller coaster world of our hearts we are invited to discover the willingness and calmness to turn toward everything that is revealed and say, "I know you."

The Wilderness of the Heart

We all encounter what the Buddha called, "the wilderness of the heart." It is the tumultuous world of our fears and doubts, the powerful emotional patterns that entangle us, the complex psychological habits, and the whole world of reactivity rooted in past experience. The wilderness of the heart holds the insistent visitors of emotional complexity that will never be dissolved by willpower, resistance, or the imposition of resolve. We are easily lost in this wilderness, feeling trapped and powerless. Simplicity, balance, and freedom seem like distant destinations.

We are emotional beings. Within our hearts we experience all the tones on the emotional scale. Rage, fear, jealousy, insecurity, hatred, and doubt all come to visit us. Moments of joy and delight, the times our hearts are filled with love and compassion, the spontaneous gestures of generosity, kindness, and warmth that move us deeply, are also part of our emotional landscape. In our spiritual path the same intensity is mirrored; we may encounter emotional ecstasy and the dark nights of the heart. There are times when we feel saturated with bliss,

THE BUDDHIST PATH TO SIMPLICITY

rapture, joy, and loving kindness. The taste of deep attention, peace, and stillness is the taste of happiness. There are also moments when we experience a seemingly bottomless pit of doubt, fear, and existential anxiety, as well as the emergence of previously unknown levels of rage, need, or terror. Our laughter and our tears have their origins within our hearts. The emergence of freedom follows a spiritual descent that touches every aspect of our being, including our emotional lives. Our emotional world invites a tender mindfulness; to understand the landscape of our hearts is to discover the source of love, generosity, compassion, and kindness.

Our emotional world can feel powerful and dangerous. There is no other dimension of our being that involves as much thinking, energy, and time. The emotions we experience can be so compelling, out of control, and unpredictable. We tend to divide our emotions into categories of positive and negative, acceptable or unacceptable. The emotions we deem to be negative or unflattering, such as greed, anger, or loneliness, we want to flee from or subdue. We regard these emotional forces as personal flaws. We attempt to cut ourselves off from emotions that are difficult, creating a dangerous schism within ourselves. Our bodies store the emotional wounds, and the emotions we have subdued out of fear may return to shatter us in moments when we are most vulnerable.

The emotions we hold to be acceptable or positive—such as love, compassion, and joy—we pursue, try to maintain, and yearn for. They delight us and connect us with others, bringing a deep sensitivity and happiness to our lives. We appreciate that the moments of greatest happiness and oneness in our lives come in those moments when are hearts are awakened. Sometimes the simplest of connections—listening to the laughter of a child or the caring words of another—have the power to touch us and remind us of the significance of heartfelt connection. When this connection feels inaccessible we may feel the need to recover once more the quality of aliveness that we treasure. Even the search for the "positive" emotions of joy and vitality can be a perilous journey. Our roller coasters become higher, our horror movies more graphic, the highs of drugs or infatuations more attractive as we search for emotional wakefulness. One day, I found myself seated on a train across from a young woman who appeared to have every visible part of her body pierced and punctured. Rings, studs, pins, and bits of metal abounded. After a time talking together, I asked her if it was painful. She answered, "Yes, but it makes me feel so alive."

We have an ambivalent relationship to our emotional landscape. We are deeply moved and enriched by our connection with joy, love, and sensitivity. We can appreciate the words of Pablo Casals when he says, "I feel the capacity to care is the thing which gives life its deepest significance and meaning." We can be terrified by the ungovernable power of the emotions that lead us to places of alienation. We can also be terrified of emotional blandness and of cultivating a path that leads to an emotional desert. At times we find ourselves in the impossible position of either succumbing to waves of emotional energy or of trying to overcome those same waves. Simplicity and awareness invite us to abandon the pathways of overcoming and succumbing, and all our artificial divisions of positive and negative, acceptable and unacceptable. In the service of freedom we are invited to explore the wilderness of our own hearts, to bring kindness and investigation, and to find awakening.

If you were to go on a hike in a wilderness and began your trek distracted and unaware—perhaps obsessing about yesterday's encounter with a friend, or daydreaming—it would not be difficult to get lost. Having gone deeply into the forest you might suddenly wake up and realize that you'd strayed from the path and lost your bearings. Waves of panic, self-blame, and desperation might swamp you. Driven by these feelings, the forest would become an enemy to escape; you would begin to flail about, yet your frantic actions would only lead to you becoming increasingly entangled in the thorns and undergrowth. Wisdom in such a moment is not to run blindly deeper into the forest, but to stand still and call forth from within a steadiness of being that allows you to listen, to discover in that stillness the way out of the wilderness. Our willingness to stand still amid emotional turbulence is the first step to discovering what it means to bring an unshakeable presence to all the storms of our lives. We are learning what it means to say, "I know you."

Finding Stillness in the Storms

We are emotional beings living in an emotional world. Stillness is rarely our first response to the waves of emotion that sweep through us. Feeling helpless within emotional storms, we come to believe that expression and action are the only means to alleviate the tensions of anger, fear, and panic. Even happiness and love appear to require action or expression for us to believe in their validity. The many forms of rage that scar our communities—road rage, supermarket rage, surf rage, institutional rage—all bear witness to the compelling power of our emotions. In the grip of an emotional storm, we feel we must do something to express it, but we are just seeking to rid ourselves of the tension surrounding the emotion. Catharsis is effective in alleviating this tension but it is a poor substitute for freedom. We honk our car horns, shout at our colleagues, feud with our neighbors, and then feel a welcome relief, yet we must also live with the consequences of our actions. We feel despair as the temporary relief wears off and we revisit the familiar patterns of tension and conflict.

Is it possible for us to find that quality of unshakeable balance in the complexity of our emotional landscape? Can we question the assumption we carry that the world and the 10 thousand things in it hold the power to enrage and depress us, or make us happy, and acknowledge that all our emotional waves begin in our own hearts and minds? If we do not question this belief, then we are a prisoner of those 10 thousand things. We delegate to them the authority to govern our emotional life and freedom.

Someone told me the story of the gamut of emotions he experienced in the aftermath of being mugged. Rage, anxiety, feelings of powerlessness, and the desire for vengeance arose in a crescendo of intensity. After a time he realized that the mugger was in charge of his life. He thought about him, obsessed about him, feared him, and opened the door for the mugger to govern his heart. As he began to explore the depth of those feelings, to accept them and befriend them, he began to reclaim his heart and freedom. Vaclav Havel, the poet and statesman, wrote, "Hatred has much in common with desire. With both comes fixation on others, dependence on them, and, in fact, a delegation of a piece of our own identity to them. The hater longs for the object of his hatred, just as the lover longs for the object of his love."

Probing Beneath the Surface

The second step in discovering emotional integrity and freedom lies in our willingness to probe beneath the concepts we use to define the emotional process. We use the words "angry," "sad," "happy," "jealous," and "fearful" to describe a many-textured experience that is impossible to describe by a single word. It is akin to describing a painting by its title. Our concepts, imposed upon a fluid, unfolding process, refer to the past and serve to interrupt the quality of attention we bring to that process in the present. We are tempted to define our identity by the concepts we impose upon our emotional life. We might refer to ourselves as an "angry" person, a "fearful" or "anxious" type, and come to believe these definitions to be the truth.

Probing beneath our concepts and descriptions, we come to understand that emotion is not a fixed preordained state arising from nowhere. All our emotions involve our bodies, feelings, memories, association, and thoughts in an unfolding interaction that is so rapid it takes remarkable attention to perceive. Some time ago, I was about to get into a taxi, when another cab roared up. The driver jumped out and began berating my cabdriver for stealing his fare. Within moments the two men were shoving each other, fighting for my suitcase, and throwing racial insults, and ended up grappling on the ground. After the fight had broken up and I was installed in the taxi, the driver began to pour out the story of his life; the endless injustices he been exposed to, the insults he'd endured, his struggles to support himself. He told me, "I am an angry man." Where was the beginning of his anger? It probably began before he was even born, an inherited legacy. Where did his anger live—in his body, in the feelings provoked by the encounter, in his thoughts and perceptions? The anger passed and another wave of emotion began—hurt, fear, and anxiety— another unfolding process.

It is the very speed with which our emotions arise and overwhelm us that makes them so daunting. Feelings, memories and associations, thoughts, reactions, and words cascade upon each other, leaving us stunned and helpless. Into this process we learn to introduce interest, investigation, and mindful awareness. The closer we can come to the beginning of an emotional wave, the greater the degree of balance and understanding we will discover. We learn to bring an alert, calm presence to the sounds, sights, thoughts, and sensations that touch us, to sense the feelings that are evoked. We notice that small feelings lead to small thoughts that arise and fade away without effort. The intense feelings we describe as loneliness, fear, anger, and excitement lead to an equal intensity in our thoughts and the degree of imprisonment we experience.

The feelings we experience determine how we feel about the world, other people, and ourselves. In the same way that we insist upon being "someone" through our self-definition, we are also prone to categorizing the world in terms of "friends" and "fiends." If we feel isolated from the world we will tend to be hostile or suspicious. If we feel happy and secure within ourselves there is little that threatens us and we tend to touch the world with kindness. In freeing ourselves from the burden of self-definition, we also liberate others from the images we have formed about them. There is the possibility of seeing anew, approaching each moment of feeling as if for the first time, and each encounter with the willingness to learn. When we cease to conceptualize ourselves or others, healing can begin. Letting go of the concepts through which we attempt to define our experience, we can explore the interwoven threads of an emotion. Sensing the changing nature of our feelings, we have the possibility of stepping away from the extremes of succumbing and overcoming to a simpler relationship of exploration and connection.

Emotional Wakefulness

In the Buddhist tradition, great attention is given to acknowledging the central role that feeling plays in life. Meditation practice is not a path inflicting an emotional lobotomy, but one of appreciating the power of our emotions as messengers of healing, compassion, and depth, as well as messengers of destruction. Instruction is given in the cultivation of loving kindness, sensitivity, forgiveness, joy, appreciation, and empathy. The Buddha once remarked that happiness is the taste of freedom. Equally, encouragement is given to understanding and releasing ourselves from greed, hatred, envy, and delusion. Superficially this appears to be a spiritual code based on "positive" and "negative." But beneath this lies the wisdom of understanding what leads to harm and what heals, a substantively different code than that of "right" and "wrong."

Simplicity does not demand that we eradicate or subdue our capacity to feel, but encourages us to liberate our emotional processes from the baggage of association, conclusion, history, fear, and obsession. An awakened heart feels deeply, loves well, treasures forgiveness and compassion, and lives with profound sensitivity. In the volumes of Buddhist texts, endless references are made to the scale of the feelings we experience, yet it is difficult to find a single word that could be translated as "emotion." Emotion is not seen as a state or an adverb, but as a process and verb that is constantly changing. No separation is made between heart, mind, and body—emotion permeates and unifies them all and in recognizing this unity we can begin to explore the body of emotion.

Emotional Habits

The wilderness of the heart is the place where we discover our capacity to bring a welcoming, unshakeable presence into our lives. Some of our emotional responses make brief appearances like sparks thrown from a fire. Other emotional patterns have a longer history and have worn deep tracks in our heart. Within these we feel the greatest sense of helplessness and confusion. They are the major building blocks of our self-image, habitual responses, and the views we have formed of life. The Buddha once said, "What we frequently think about and dwell upon becomes the inclination of our heart." If we harbor resentment and obsess about the long list of injustices and hurt that have scarred our lives, bitterness and mistrust form the landscape of our hearts and minds. In turn, this becomes our way of interpreting the world. If we dwell repeatedly upon the disappointments and failures, this too shapes our heart and mind and we live with cynicism and doubt. Nurturing calmness, understanding, and trust within ourselves impacts directly upon our way of seeing each person and encounter entering our lives.

The familiar grooves of our emotions hold an almost fatal attraction for us, overriding our intention to see anew, to live with openness and balance. If you had a favorite walk, visited it repeatedly, and yet always walked in the same footprints you had made in the past, you would soon to begin to make an impression on the landscape. Your path would first turn into a furrow in the ground and then a ditch. Most of us would not willingly throw ourselves headfirst into a ditch. Yet with the deep grooves worn in our hearts, we find ourselves falling in, at times throwing ourselves in, simply because we do not know the other pathways to walk.

The emotional patterns in which we feel the most stuck and powerless are the very places that invite the greatest patience, compassion, and transformation. It is possible to be reluctant to seek transformation within emotional habits, even when we know they are painful. We experience the contractedness and suffering of our rage, but fear letting go of it. Who would we be without our rage? Would the person who has harmed us get away with their actions? We may feel the deep sorrow that feelings of shame and worthlessness bring, yet to nurture another way of being in our lives involves risk and exposure. Greed is an uncomfortable experience, yet the second serving of food tastes wonderful. Emotional freedom begins with our wholehearted commitment to freeing ourselves from sorrow and to deeply caring for our own well-being.

Pathways to Emotional Balance

When we find ourselves in the grip of an emotional storm, it is helpful to reflect on the qualities of heart that are obviously absent. In the midst of anger or judgment, our hearts become closed, our minds contracted. In these moments it helps to *cultivate* an intentional sense of loving kindness and compassion for ourselves and others, to nurture a conscious forgiveness. In moments of great confusion or anxiety, we can return to the simplicity of feeling our body, sensing our breath, and the contact of our feet with the earth. When we feel lost in storms of grief, loneliness, and alienation, what a difference it makes to find the ways and places that remind us of the possibility of joy.

The pathway of *wise avoidance* can, in moments of emotional confusion, be our lifeline to simplicity and calm. There are familiar pathways of self-judgment, greed, and bitterness we have traveled a thousand times before. We know the history that lies behind those pathways, we know the suffering of being lost on them, and we know the destination they lead to. It may not be a lack of understanding that inclines us to follow those pathways, but simply ingrained habit. There is wisdom in withdrawing our consent, finding the calm and clear intention to say "No" to sorrow. If our leg were broken, there would be a limit to how much learning we would gain through observing the pain. There would be a point where wise action would involve taking the appropriate steps to bring the pain to an end. Wise avoidance may involve taking our attention out of the familiar groove of our habits. A moment of deep listening to the song of a bird, reflecting upon the nature of calmness, moving our bodies, can bring the space we need to see a habit as a habit that we need not be bound to.

Restraint can be a great ally in finding freedom and simplicity within emotional complexity. Superficially, restraint appears contrary to freedom, but only if we interpret freedom as permission. Seeing ourselves about to dive into familiar responses of impatience, judgment, or blame, the willingness to pause for a moment, to sense the driving power of emotion in our bodies, to honor stillness, enables us to find balance. When living in the mountains in India we were often pestered by stray dogs which haunted our doorways. One day I found myself picking up a stone to frighten away a particularly persistent dog scavenging in our garbage. Just as I was about to throw the stone, my teacher appeared walking up the pathway. My first response, being an aspiring spiritual seeker, was to feel a tremendous sense of shame and failure. Instead of scolding me, my teacher invited me to see the dog as a being who, in the past or future, might be my child. How would I want to treat it?

Investigation is crucial to bringing light and simplicity into our emotional storms. We can learn to bring the willingness to see what is actually happening within the turbulence of our emotions, to probe beneath the concepts and images, and explore the feelings. "This *is* sadness, grief, anger, jealousy" is a very different way of appreciating our experience than "I *am* sad, bereft, angry, jealous." As we pay close attention, not fearing or denying anything, we see the way in which feelings and thoughts are constantly changing, impacting on our bodies and minds. We learn to say, "I know you," and understand that there is nothing that is unwelcome. Learning to release the ownership, the "I" that is invested in our emotions, we understand that they hold no intrinsic power to shape the landscape of our hearts and minds. Their only power is given to them through our codes of "right" and "wrong," the "self" we invest in them, and the fears we surround them with. Investigation reveals the suffering that is born of being lost, and that the willingness to release ourselves from imprisonment is the deepest gift of compassion we can offer to ourselves.

In our darkest times of being lost or overpowered there is also wisdom in *reaching out* to ask for help. The mentors, wise friends, and guides in our lives who treasure our well-being, are allies to call upon in the moments of greatest pain. Asking for help is a gesture of humility, the acknowledgement that we cannot always do everything alone, that there are times when our will is simply not enough to bring about the freedom we treasure.

A path of genuine awakening is a path of growing increasingly alive and aware in our emotions. As we learn to release the stories, interpretations, and resistance that camouflage our emotional life, our emotions become more accessible and simple—fear is just fear, loneliness just loneliness, anger just anger, joy just joy—thus inviting exploration and understanding. Waves of feeling are no longer frozen by our attempts to define them—they arise and ebb away. We learn to find refuge in stillness and calm. Diving more and more deeply into stillness, there are times when deeply buried emotional wounds and memories arise; we learn to receive them and find freedom within them.

Probing the life of our emotions, we also come to understand the underlying presence of fear. Heidegger once said, "Anxiety is there, it is only sleeping, its breath quivers perpetually through our being." What is anger but the fear of being hurt? What is greed but the fear of not having enough? What is loneliness but the fear of abandonment? Within jealousy we see the fear of being judged inferior. Within dependency we sense the fear of loneliness. A Christian mystic suggested, "Anxiety is the mood of ignorance." In different words we come to see that fear is the inevitable consequence of alienation from a true understanding of interconnectedness and life. The creative power of our emotions to heal, to serve, to love, to empathize, and live with joy is born of releasing this alienation. Our hearts can sing when they are no longer burdened by fear.

The Journey from the Known to the Unknown

Fear is the passageway between the known and the unknown. It is a passageway we are asked to walk through as we go beneath the concepts, labels, and images that make our world familiar and safe. In deeper levels of meditation there is an existential fear that is touched upon. This fear has no specific object; it is not fear of the dark, of people, of failure, but the fear that comes to visit us when it is no longer possible to define ourselves or anything in our world. We are not asked to endure this fear, survive it, or suffer with it, but to welcome it and explore it, leave it if we wish and understand that it is the forerunner of freedom. Fearlessness does not mean that fear never arises, but it entails our willingness to turn toward it, understand it, and find within it the simplicity of being present.

Walking the passageway between the known and the unknown involves the faith that it is possible for us to be free and awake. There is a story of an atheist who, out walking one day, fell off the edge of a cliff. As he tumbled downward he caught hold of a small tree—there he hung with rocks a thousand feet below, knowing he wasn't able to hold on much longer. Then an idea came, "God," he shouted with all his might. Silence. No response. "God," he shouted again, "If you are real, save me and I promise I'll believe in you forever." Silence again. He almost let go in shock as he heard a mighty voice boom across the canyon. "That's what they all say when they're in trouble." "No, God, no," he shouted out, more hopeful now. "I'm not like the others. I've already begun to believe now I've heard your voice. All you have to do is save me and I shall proclaim your name to the ends of the earth." "Very well," said the voice, "I shall save you. Let go of the branch." "Let go of the branch?" yelled the distraught man, "Do you think I'm crazy?"

Finding simplicity within our hearts asks us to let go, just as the emergence of simplicity in all of our lives asks us to let go. We let go of the stories, the beliefs, the fears, and our hearts learn to sing. Wandering in the wilderness, our sense of being lost ends the moment we find traces of the path. The wilderness is no longer an enemy. We appreciate the towering trees as well as the thorns and brambles. We are able to say, "I know you" and discover an unshakeable presence.

GUIDED MEDITATION

Take a few moments to reflect on the emotions that hold the greatest power in your life, the places where you most easily become lost. Invite them into your heart, whether they are anger, loneliness, fear, jealousy, or self-hatred. Sense how they feel in your body. Does your chest or belly start to tighten, your breathing become shallower? Be aware of the stories that accompany these feelings, the memories of the past, fears for the future. Sense the feelings that lie at the heart of the stories.

Explore what happens if you bring your attention back into your body and be aware of how your body responds to those emotions. Explore with your attention those places in your body that are registering emotion. Sense how a sensitive, gentle attention that makes no demands begins to soften the areas of tightness and contractedness.

As you are increasingly present within the emotional life of your body, sense how the insistent nature of the stories, memories, and fears begins to soften. Simplify, welcome, and explore what it might mean to be emotionally alive, yet awake and present.

As you experience these emotions, experiment with taking your attention to listening; be aware of the sounds near and far. Open your eyes and appreciate the space around you, feel the sensations of your body touching the earth. Come back to the sense of the emotion within you, surrounding it with a calm acceptance, a warmth of heart.

Take a few moments to reflect on the emotions that nurture you, sustain you, and heal you—the experiences of joy, happiness, and peace. Invite them into your heart and sense them in your body. More thoughts and memories may come. Let them be, not being lost anywhere.

Ask yourself what is needed to hold both the experience of joy and the experience of sorrow. Ask yourself what is needed to discover freedom and simplicity within your heart. Hold these questions without demanding an answer, but as an open invitation offered to yourself.

effort

You must be the change you wish to see in the world.

MAHATMA GANDHI

BESIDE a waterfall on the banks of the River Ganges lives an Indian sadhu, a holy man, renowned for his spiritual depth and power. Pilgrims come from around the world to pay their respects and spend time in his presence. Each morning the sadhu arises and goes to stand beside the waterfall. Placing his hands together, he bows to the waterfall and whispers, "Welcome." Throughout the day, he stands still beside the gushing waters. As the day ends, once more he bows deeply to the waterfall with gratitude, saying, "Well done." For years this simple vigil has been both his practice and his teaching.

There are no long discourses, initiations, or rituals, yet for those who come to spend time in his presence there is a powerful teaching about effort, vision, perseverance, and simplicity. Superficially this may appear a shallow, aimless, or irrelevant life. There is meager evidence of goals achieved, results produced, or an engagement with the grist and suffering of life. For someone whose life is compelled by pressure, deadlines, and expectations, this may appear an idyllic existence. For the ambitious person, who measures their worth through attainment and accolade, this may appear a pointless life. Yet within this paradigm of the silent vigil by the waterfall there is held some of the deepest paradoxes of spiritual life.

What effort does it require to hold that posture of alert and welcoming presence day after day? What qualities of perseverance and steadiness are needed to be still and balanced in this changing and fragile world? What kind of commitment is needed to trust that the simple observing of a waterfall offers everything that is needed for awakening? What depth of nonattachment is required simply to be a presence in the presence of life, without the assurance of progress through signposts and attainment. In his vigil, the sadhu embodies heroic effort, yet he remains unmoving. His practice expresses profound dedication, engagement, and attention, yet he is going nowhere. Perhaps through his story we learn that the path is also the destination, the means are not separate from the ends.

Attainment and Immanence

Within all Buddhist traditions we are faced with two, apparently contradictory, visions of the spiritual journey. These visions are clearly illustrated through the story of Hui Neng. As a young man, born into an impoverished family in China, Hui Neng long aspired to become part of the local monastery. Because of his lowly birth and his lack of education and social graces, he was repeatedly refused entry. Months passed with him lingering outside the monastery gate, begging to be accepted under any conditions. Realizing the young man was not going to go away, one of the senior monks took pity on him and agreed that he could join the community as a humble kitchen worker. Time passed with Hui Neng cleaning the rice, sweeping the floors, and serving the elder monks and nuns. The abbot of the temple was nearing the end of his life and was urged to determine who would be his successor. To assess the wisdom of the monks and nuns in the community, he invited them to write a verse illustrating the depth of their understanding. Hui Neng, living in the shadows of the community, was not included in the invitation. Verse after verse was written upon the monastery wall, yet the majority of the community assumed that the leadership would automatically pass to the eldest monk, long devoted to the master and a conscientious practitioner. With great respect he was invited to write his verse of understanding and upon the wall inscribed,

The body is a bodhi tree,
The mind a mirror bright,
Carefully we polish them hour by hour,
And let no dust alight.

His verse was greeted with great admiration and acclaim, and his promotion to abbot seemed assured. That night, as the monastery slept, Hui Neng rose from his pallet in the kitchen to write his own verse upon the wall. He laboriously scribbled,

There is no bodhi tree,
Nor is there mirror bright,
Buddha nature shines clear and bright,
Where can dust alight

The first verse presents the journey of awakening as an arduous path, filled with perils, that requires unrelenting effort. It presents a path that requires time, where result is dependant upon personal responsibility and where the destination is perceived as distant and separate. It is a path of heroic effort, the journey of the warrior.

The verse of Hui Neng offers a radically different version of the path where awakening is imminent, with no obstacles to be overcome and no goal to reach for. It presents qualities of effortlessness and ease. These two approaches to awakening have been the source of endless debate within spiritual communities and they hold the potential to puzzle and confuse us in our own journey.

Each of these visions offer different understandings of what kind of effort is truly needed for us to awaken and to find ease and simplicity within our own hearts and journeys. When awakening is perceived as a distant goal, separate from where we are, we come to believe that heroic effort is required of us. But if we accept the vision that there is nowhere for us to go and nothing for us to achieve, it seems obvious that effort is irrelevant. One great master spoke of effort, saying that in this journey we must be prepared to make the effort that leads us to "sweat beads." Another great sage remarked that there will come a time in our lives when we look back on all of our heroic efforts as "futile actions performed in a dream."

The Art of Awakening

Awakening is an art and like any other art it requires a delicate blend of love and discipline. When we undertake any venture in our lives, whether it is climbing a mountain, learning to play a musical instrument, overturning injustice or bringing our potential to be free to fulfillment, it is the love and discipline we find within ourselves that translates our dreams into reality. Martin Luther King Jr. and Nelson Mandela shared a dream of equality and freedom. Mother Theresa held a dream where the outcasts from society could find a place to live and die with dignity and love. Mahatma Gandhi and His Holiness the Dalai Lama envisioned their people living free from oppression and injustice. It is not just the capacity to dream that has brought to fulfillment the radical social and spiritual transformations in the world, but the capacity to blend vision with the effort needed to bring dreams to fulfillment.

It is not just the great saints, heroes, and heroines who dream of freedom and who change their world profoundly with their vision. The parents who fight against drug addiction in their community, the teacher who seeks to awaken aspiration in the midst of deprivation, the migrant laborer who demands justice, these all share in a common aspiration—reaching for what is possible. We too have our own dreams, our own sense of vision. Our hearts long for peace, simplicity, intimacy, and freedom. We envision a way of being in which we are no longer haunted by struggle, confusion, and conflict. We sense within ourselves the sparks of compassion, generosity, and wisdom. Our dreams are important to us; they are the catalyst that moves us to begin a path of awakening. Vision is a combination of divine discontent and divine curiosity. Divine discontent is the unwillingness to resign ourselves to a life that features repetitive cycles of conflict and struggle, punctuated by moments of peace, as being the only life we are eligible for. Divine curiosity is the willingness to probe beneath the surface of our mind and life to discover the simplicity, peace, and freedom we sense is possible. The Buddha called the vision of freedom the "one fortunate attachment."

Love and Discipline

Vision is about love in its deepest sense. It is the vision of what we hold to be possible for us as human beings that sets the direction of our thinking and action. Vision is the frame for the direction of our lives. To awaken to what is possible for us we are asked to examine what it is that is most important to us. We are invited to explore what it is that sustains and nurtures us, what moves us to live with integrity and kindness, and what genuinely frees us. So much that we can dedicate our lives to, in the realm of possessions, attainments, and experience, will crumble in time. To discover peace we are asked to love peace; to discover simplicity we are invited to be passionate about simplicity; to be deeply awake we are asked for a profound dedication.

Love needs to be balanced with discipline. Discipline is an unfashionable word, evoking memories of a harshness and imposition that confines or suppresses—we fear this discipline, aware of its lethal consequences. Awakening our hearts and minds asks for a discipline of a different order—a discipline born of love, of vision, and intuition. Awakening to our lives asks for commitment; not a commitment to a guru, ideology, or tradition, but a commitment to ourselves. Every effort we make in our lives to awaken, to be present, and to honor our intuition of wholeness, is an expression of this commitment and love. Every effort we make to heal division and nurture intimacy is an embodiment of vision. Each moment we seek to understand and heal the causes of conflict and sorrow, we are honoring vision and wise effort.

Joyful Effort

Wise effort is the effort to be awake, mindful, and present in all the circumstances and encounters of our lives. It is not just effort that translates our dreams into reality, but joyful effort. Joyful effort arises from two foundations—aspiration and self-confidence. The intuition of our own possibility to be whole, free, loving human beings needs to be matched with an appreciation of our capacity to listen deeply, to learn, and to rely upon ourselves. No one travels a path of awakening where there is undiluted bliss, tranquility, or transcendent experience. There will be countless moments of frustration, feelings of getting nowhere, times of meeting inner demons. There will be moments when our inner descent bears little resemblance to anyone else's and we are filled with uncertainty. In the moments of adversity, vision is strengthened by self-confidence. Dorothea Brandt reminds us, "Go confidently in the direction of your dreams. Act as though it was impossible to fail."

Spiritual investigation questions all the beliefs, self-images, cultural assumptions, and conclusions we have accumulated without condition. Countless resistance, doubts, fears, and anxieties come to the surface. At times we recoil from them, feel overwhelmed by them, or experience the ground of our being crumbling beneath us. It is here that self-confidence and inner assurance rescue us from despair. A young boy once asked his mother, "What would you do if you imagined you were surrounded by a pack of hungry tigers with no one to save you?" His mother answered, "I don't know. What would you do?" He answered, "I'd stop pretending." Without self-confidence or inner trust we imagine our tigers to be more solid and powerful than they actually are. We invest them with the authority to define the quality of our inner environment and our responses. Perhaps they are not so immovable, impenetrable, or powerful as we imagine. Wise effort is the willingness to turn towards our tigers, greet them with confidence, and explore their reality.

Wise effort, joyful effort, is the effort to engage with everything that is presented to us from our inner and outer world. As long as we imagine our tigers to be so powerful, our responses to them will become increasingly complex. We evolve strategies to tame them, bargain with them, subdue them, or overcome them. Wise effort is born of the simple willingness to learn from them, to embrace and accept them.

Within this wise effort we discover a quality of effortlessness and joy as we discover that the effort to engage is the effort that disempowers our tigers and empowers ourselves. At times this effort will resemble the kindly presence of a benevolent grandmother who embraces the sorrow and confusion of her grandchild. Gentleness, interest, and compassion allow us to find the inner space to accommodate those thoughts we previously felt overpowering. At other times, to stay engaged we need to find the courage of a warrior to remain steady and connected. It takes great courage to be honest with ourselves and to open our hearts to the reality of sorrow, conflict, and struggle. The habits of avoidance, disengagement, suppression, or fantasy may be the most powerful of our tigers. Genuine

effort, and the understanding it evokes, is learned most deeply
in the school of adversity. Arnold Bennett remarked, "It is
easier to go down a hill than up, but the view is from the top."

Wherever we are in our lives, on the top of a mountain or
in a crowd, the one thing we cannot escape from is our own
consciousness. Whatever we experience in life, whether joy or
sorrow, ease or challenge, our consciousness is our companion.
We cannot always control the world or the life experiences
that come to us, and we cannot transcend our own consciousness. Yet we are not powerless; we hold within ourselves the
capacity for listening, learning, and freedom. Our consciousness that holds the capacity for fear, confusion, complexity, and
doubt also holds the seeds of courage, clarity, simplicity, and
trust. Not understanding this, we search the world, engage in
endless self-improvement, and adopt countless strategies of
modification, seeking to find the fulfillment of happiness, ease,
and simplicity outside of ourselves. As one master put it, "The
treasure you seek for lies within, so why do you go begging
from door to door?" Wise effort, simple effort returns us to
engage with this consciousness and this moment, understanding that confusion and simplicity lie in the same place.

Just as we cannot divorce ourselves from the quality of our
consciousness, it is impossible to divorce ourselves from all the
changes, encounters, people, and circumstances in this life.
There is no alternative to engaging with life—whether we do
so consciously or unconsciously, joyfully or reluctantly, rests
upon the capacity for joyful effort we discover inwardly. An
inmate trying to practice meditation on death row told me his

practice was obstructed by the circumstances he was in; if only he was out in the world his meditation would be much clearer. Countless people living a householder's life, endeavoring to sustain wakefulness and depth, comment that they would be far more awake and peaceful if they were in a monastery. Go to any monastery and you will encounter monks and nuns who complain that their practice would definitely improve if the food and weather were better, the monastery were quieter, and they had more amicable companions. Wherever we are in this life, delusion and enlightenment reside in the same place. Until we recognize this reality, the efforts we make will continue to be complex and frustrating.

Transformation

When the Buddha arose from his vigil under the Bodhi tree on the night of his awakening he said, "I gained absolutely nothing from complete unexcelled enlightenment. This is why it is complete unexcelled enlightenment." He then went on to teach a path saying, "There is this shore and there is the other shore and the path that carries us safely over." All great spiritual traditions speak of the possibilities of profound peace, liberation, wisdom, and heartfelt compassion that are immanent within each of us. Possibilities not only promised to the special, saintly, and holy who have the ideal life and personal attributes of greatness, but possibilities held in each human consciousness. Our capacity for delusion, greed, anger, and confusion are also spoken of at great length. We all know what this shore can feel like—to be lost in whirlwinds of alienation, need, and aversion are familiar experiences. Vision leads us to look for a path to the other shore.

None of us travels a path of awakening in order to stay the same—we have little interest in becoming more intimately acquainted with a chaotic mind, a complaining body, or a tumultuous heart. When we begin a path we look for change and transformation, to realize the possibilities of the freedom from which we feel separated. Every spiritual path offers direction and invites effort, focus, and dedication. No one outside of ourselves, no matter how loving or wise, can cultivate this path for us. It can only be cultivated in the midst of this life, body, heart, and mind. There is not a better moment than this one in which to awaken, nor a more fertile moment to nurture sensitivity, simplicity, and depth.

Unwise Effort

It is in the apparent gap between this shore, our present reality, and the other shore, the ideals we seek to realize, that we can fall into confusion and complexity. Ideals become goals, goals invite striving, and striving becomes a rejection of the present. The prince Siddhartha spent years abusing his body, rejecting the world, and cultivating ascetic practices that scarred him in the pursuit of transcendence, until he finally understood that the liberation he sought would not be found somewhere other than where he was. We too can transfer from our lives beliefs that bring to our journey both a sense of exaggerated responsibility and an aversion for ourselves and our lives. We may believe that change relies entirely upon us, on the effort we make, and the heroic attempts we make to overcome the obstacles in our way. We may be seeking perfection rather than liberation. Signposts and signals of progress assume great significance. We have "good" meditations and "bad" meditations, judged by whether our experience conforms to our images and expectations. Suffering may even be interpreted as a sign of progress, of truly "getting to grips" with things. Our spiritual path is turned into a battlefield; challenges and adversity become the enemies to subdue. Rather than opening up to what is in each moment with a willingness to learn, we become increasingly defensive and suspicious of our own being. Rarely is this a joyful effort: it is work, a project, a mission. The Buddha once said, "This is a path of happiness leading to the highest happiness and the highest happiness is peace."

How do we know what is unskillful effort? Simply whenever happiness too becomes a goal, separate and apart from where we are. We can feel the consequences of our striving in the tension in our bodies and the resistance in our minds. We know it is unskillful because the dualities of "winning" and "losing," "good" and "bad," "worthy" and "unworthy" are constant companions in our minds. We know it is unskillful because we are trying to get out of a life that simply won't go away. Complex and unskillful effort is primarily born of anxiety. We fear that if this heroic effort is not made we will sink into lethargy, be consumed by our shadows, or fail.

Wise Effort

Wise, simple effort is an antidote to the spiritual malaise that dampens the realization of our vision and intuition, a malaise that creates its own delusions. Spiritual malaise can disguise itself as effortlessness, yet it is permeated by delusion. Deep inner feelings of worthlessness and inadequacy convince us that peace, wisdom, and liberation are not open to us; too many endeavors in our lives have resulted in a failure that confirms our inadequacy. We become cynical or spiritually depressed. There is a malaise that comes when our ambitions remain unrealized and we cannot identify progress. There is a malaise that is evoked when our infatuation with those things that appear to offer immediate gratification is greater than our vision of enduring happiness. We tell ourselves that renunciation is a good theory, but the second plate of food is too inviting. We agree that boundless loving kindness is a wonderful philosophy, but it may involve forgiving the person who has tormented us through our lives. Mired in this malaise, awakening seems like too much effort. Spiritual malaise is a powerful force compelling us into passivity and resignation, or into ambition and forcing— both inevitably end in frustration and despair.

A great Zen master once said, "Meditation is not a way to enlightenment, nor is it a method of achieving anything at all. It is peace and blessedness in itself." With wise and simple effort we learn to walk our path and be awake to our lives without seeking anything apart from what can be discovered here and now. We learn the art of embodying our vision in every step of our path. Treasuring peace, we seek to discover peace in adversity; treasuring compassion, we learn to listen deeply to our life. Committing ourselves to being awake we bring an illuminating attention to those places in our lives where the possibilities of depth are camouflaged by habit or disconnection. We treat no thing and no one in our lives as being unworthy of our wholehearted attention and we learn to live with reverence. We begin to understand that joyful effort, simple effort takes many forms and we learn to explore them. The seeds of awakening lie within us, their cultivation relies upon our dedication. A Zen master remarked, "Everything is perfect, but there is a lot of room for improvement."

Another Zen master was invited to a great Catholic monastery to give instruction in Zen practice. He exhorted the community to meditate and try to solve the *koan* or question with great energy and zeal, advising that if they meditated with full-hearted effort, true understanding would come to them. One old monk raised his hand, "Master," he said, "Our way of prayer is different to this. We have been meditating and praying in the simplest fashion without effort, waiting instead to be illuminated by the grace of God. In Zen is there anything like this illuminating grace that comes to one uninvited?" The Zen master laughed. "In Zen," he said, "we believe that God has already done his share."

With wise effort we embrace the paradox of immanence and transformation, understanding it to be a mystery rather than a contradiction. Vision teaches us to probe beneath the surface of conflict, confusion, and alienation to discover peace, clarity, and wholeness. Effort is made, not to transport us to some other destination, but to return us to the simple truth of each moment. Wise and simple effort involves equal parts of cultivation and letting go, understanding what is needed in each moment to return us to wakefulness. Wise effort encourages us to open the doors to the rooms in our heart that have been closed, to bring steadiness to the moments when we quake with doubt or anxiety, to come closer to the terrors we have previously fled, and to bring investigation to the places in our lives and hearts that feel shrouded in fog or confusion. This is not a project but an engagement. A wise teacher advised on the importance of the attitude from which our efforts spring—to be as curious, light, interested, and attentive as a child setting out on an adventure.

There are psychological theories that profess that our character, personality, and ways of thinking, seeing, and feeling, are formed and hardened in our early adolescence; through the rest of our lives we simply learn strategies and formulas to make our character acceptable in the world. It is suggested that if by our early teens we are fearful, greedy, ambitious, angry, passive, loving, or open, then that is who we will be until we die, with only minor modifications possible. It is a theory curiously at odds with the teachings of transformation held within great spiritual traditions, and with the experience of countless people who explore those teachings in depth. At the heart of a vision of awakening is a simple truth—that just because something has a long history, it is not a life sentence. Our capacity to be awake in our lives means that transformation is always possible.

There is mystery within transformation. We cannot always predict how the power of inner stillness and life experience will awaken us. Just as the young prince Siddhartha was startled into wakefulness through his encounters with sickness, aging, and death, we too can be startled into wakefulness through our own encounters with change, birth, wisdom, uncertainty, and loss. When our worlds fall apart and our certainties are dissolved, we receive powerful invitations to awaken to our lives. Alongside this mystery lives our path, a conscious intentional cultivation of investigation, stillness, and transformation.

Cultivating a Mind and Heart of Wisdom

The first of the wise efforts found in the Buddhist tradition is the effort to foster, nurture, and enhance the skillful, beautiful, wholesome qualities of our being that are present within our heart and mind. Calmness, patience, generosity, loving kindness, and compassion arise and we learn to be intimate with them. They are the seeds of great depth, connectedness, and openheartedness that ask for our care and exploration. How do we experience them in our body and mind? How do they change our perception of and relationship to people, events, and ourselves? In exploring these qualities we come to understand the happiness, peace, and simplicity that follow in their wake. In learning to give attention to these qualities, to honor and appreciate them without grasping, they grow and deepen.

Too often we discount ourselves or dismiss the presence of the beautiful and wholesome within us as accidents we do not deserve. Speaking once with a woman on a meditation retreat who carried with her a long history of unworthiness, she shyly reported encounters with a deep stillness and profound calm in her meditation. She quickly undermined her report with the words, "I doubt if it was truly genuine. It was probably just the menopause." For a child to grow into a sense of her own beauty and completeness she needs to be honored. For the budding shoots of a plant to flower they need tender care and attention. For us to trust in our own capacity for healing, transformation, and freedom, we are asked to honor, foster and enhance the loveliness within ourselves.

Letting go of Unskilful States

The second of the wise and skillful efforts is to learn to release ourselves from the confusing, unskillful, or unwholesome states that drive us into alienation, confusion, and complexity. Greed, anger, hatred, jealousy, or obsession are not to be released because they are bad, unspiritual, or unworthy, but simply because they lead only further to sorrow, fear, and conflict. We learn not to judge ourselves, nor to shout at ourselves to "let go," but to explore these experiences gently in our body, heart, mind, and life. With clear and kind attention we probe beneath their surface to understand the confusion from which they are born and to acknowledge where they take us. These qualities do not release themselves because we push them away, ignore them, or command their demise. The effort to engage, explore, and investigate, to embrace them in a kind and loving attention, is the effort that transforms them. Wise and simple effort is the effort to heal, clarify, and simplify. We bring that quality of effort to all the places in our lives and hearts where there is division, hatred, confusion, and struggle, and we ask, "Where does the healing begin?" Increasingly, we understand that it begins in our own hearts, born of our own effort and vision.

Awakening the Dormant Qualities Within

The third of the wise and skillful efforts is the effort to encourage, inspire, and cultivate the emergence of the healing, lovely, and wise qualities of heart and mind that lie dormant within us. Vision reminds us of our capacity to listen deeply, to be aware, and to realize our own potential for greatness of heart and mind. It is wise effort to nudge those seeds of potential from dormancy into life. In the midst of our impatience in a traffic jam, we surprise ourselves by cultivating loving kindness. As we turn away with aversion from the person begging from us on the street, we pause for a moment and remember the power of compassion. As we feel ourselves becoming seduced by our inner stories of resentment or bitterness, we remind ourselves of our own capacity to find balance and calm. In the moments when we feel most despairing, powerless, or confused, we remember that we have the capacity to listen deeply and find connectedness. We remind ourselves of the simplicity, calm, and peace possible, and we cultivate them.

Avoiding Unskilful states

The last of the four wise efforts is to avoid the unskillful, unwholesome, and unfree states of body and mind that have not arisen. Wise avoidance is neither aversion nor rejection, but the simple recognition that not all experiences or circumstances in life are conducive to our well-being. A young man on retreat spoke of the dilemma and resistance he faced each time he left a retreat and returned to his job that involved experimenting on animals in a cosmetics factory. Each night, he said, he came home increasingly distressed and conflicted, yet wrongly believed that with enough equanimity he would be able to show up for work each morning without a struggle. We may not be faced with overt conflicts in our lives, yet we appreciate that there are times when habit takes us to places that are far from where we wish to be. We may find ourselves dulling our hearts with over-consumption, mortifying ourselves with excessive stimulation, and be aware of the countless ways we undermine our inner confidence, clarity, and openness. Habit exists strongly in the pathways we tread in our hearts and minds that erode our inner well-being. Habits of judgment, fantasy, and obsession dull and cloud our capacity for trust, simplicity, and wholeness. We learn wise avoidance in the understanding that those well-worn pathways no longer offer further understanding or well-being.

Wise and simple effort is to awaken understanding, and understanding is the mother of transformation. Wise effort is also needed to comprehend the implications of the understanding that deepens within us and to embody it in each moment of our lives. If we truly understand what leads to sorrow and what leads to happiness, we are invited to turn toward our lives and explore where we are fostering pathways of sorrow and where the pathways of happiness lie. Insight becomes meaningless if we continue to walk pathways of confusion. We are invited to heal the rifts in our relationships and communities, to commit ourselves to patience and generosity, and find the courage to speak what is most true. If we understand the implications of greed, resentment, and jealousy we are asked to make the effort to live in a new way, based on forgiveness, empathy, and appreciation. If we deeply understand the nature of change, we are asked to let go of everything that we cling to most tightly. We are invited to engage with our lives.

A spiritual path in not just an inner life, secluded and separate from the world we live in. It is not only a path of inner transformation and personal well-being, but a path dedicated to the transformation of all sorrow and to the well-being of all life. The wisdom born of our effort to be inwardly awake and aware expresses itself in wise action, speech, and choice. Huango Po, a Chinese master advised, "Do not consent to being bound by the events of your life, but never withdraw from them. Only by acting thus can you merit the title of a 'liberated being.'"

GUIDED MEDITATION

Take a few moments to reflect on the quality of effort you bring to your life and meditation.

Do you see them as battlegrounds? Do you strive too much, and see fulfillment as a distant goal? Are you guided by a deep intuition of the possibilities of freedom available to you, or by fears and "shoulds?" What kind of effort do you bring to the tigers in your heart and life? What difference would it make to open to them, listen deeply, and appreciate the understanding they offer? What would you need to cultivate or let go of to be genuinely more awake?

With a gentle attention, ask yourself if there is an equal balance of inner confidence and vision. In the midst of tension or struggle, ask yourself where calm and peace truly lie. In the midst of confusion or heaviness, take a moment to listen wholeheartedly to the sounds around you, to the life of your own body and being, to forge the small bridges of connectedness. In the moments of being lost in the past or future, in fantasy, or any whirlwind of the mind, explore what it means just to feel your body wholeheartedly, to see just one leaf fully, to sense the underlying feelings beneath the surface of the storm. Explore what it means just to be awake, to be mindful, to be here.

speech

Take time to listen to what is said without words,
To obey the law too subtle to be written,
To worship the unnamable,
And to embrace the unformed.

LAO-TZU

THERE are people who love silence, are at ease in silence, and content in solitude. There are people who love talking, delight in conversing, and seek the company of others. However, it is a rare person who understands what it is to speak wisely, who is at ease with silence, and who finds equal joy in solitude and in company. To understand wise speech is a gift, and it calls for immense mindfulness to know when to speak, when to be silent, how to speak words that touch the heart of another, and how to listen.

Our words are our thoughts with wings. We open our mouths and our minds fly out. There are times when we are startled, even shocked, at the words that have flown from our lips. At times we speak and, in listening to ourselves, wonder whose voice we are speaking with; it sounds like our mother, our father, or a voice we have inherited from a stranger. In other moments we discover we can find just the words that are needed to heal, to convey love and tenderness. Most often they are words born of inner stillness and deep listening. The agitated mind is the forerunner of agitated speech; the mind of calmness and simplicity is the forerunner of speech that communicates openness and sensitivity

Before we speak we think; before we think we feel; how we feel about anything is linked to our past experience, memories, and preferences, to our conditioning and the state of our mind in that moment. Learning to take care of our speech is learning to take care of our thoughts, feelings, and mind. Caring for ourselves, we take care of all the minds, feelings, and life of those who we impact with our speech. We learn to cultivate loving kindness, compassion, wisdom, and simplicity as the seeds from which our speech is born. We are likely to find that in doing so we speak less and listen more.

We should never underestimate the power of our speech. The words we speak are pivotal in the kind of relationships we form and how we touch the hearts of others. Unwise speech causes heartbreak and separation; it makes enemies and creates fear. Wise speech has the power to heal division, to foster love and trust, and leads to intimacy. Our words are vehicles of communication; what we communicate is far deeper and more complex than just the concepts that are uttered. Our words are weapons for the realization of justice, truth, and dignity, just as they can be weapons that incite violence, destruction, and alienation. Through the words we speak we can change another person's world in a moment. Words of cruelty, harshness, dismissiveness, and anger linger long in the heart of the person they are spoken to. We carry deep wounds in our hearts that have been inflicted by words of anger. Words of love, tenderness, and kindness are urgently needed in a world saturated by so many unwise and divisive words. The realization of peace in our world, our communities, families, and relationships rests upon each of us learning to speak with wisdom.

Wise speech is both an ethical and spiritual exploration. Committing ourselves to wise speech, we learn to listen inwardly to the words beneath the words. Attentive to the feelings, intentions, and thoughts beneath our words, we learn to cultivate the compassion, integrity, and kindness that bring harmony to our relationships and to our own mind. Wise speech is rooted in compassion and integrity. It protects the people we speak to and protects our own heart from guilt and remorse. In learning to listen both outwardly and inwardly before we speak, we begin to appreciate the strength and the fragility of the human heart.

An Authentic Voice

Exploring the path of wise speech is an invitation to find our own voice—a voice of authenticity rooted in our personal experience and innate wisdom. In fostering our voice we release the countless voices we have inherited in our lives that bear with them their own values and expectations. The voices of judgment, ambition, perfection, fear, and abandonment shout within us, diminishing our capacity for listening. Throughout our lives we are deafened by the voices that exhort us to compete, achieve, possess, and judge—commands and exhortations that inform the voice we speak with.

A voice rooted in wisdom treasures truthfulness, respect, and compassion, and it honors our interconnectedness. Wise speech is directly linked to integrity and wise understanding. We learn to speak the words that we would wish to hear, to speak words that we do not regret, simply and wisely. Our words will come to express the values we care about most deeply, and communicate them in a way that can be heard by others. We could think of a simple reflection. If you were to meet with your dearest friend for a few last moments, what is it you would wish to say and wish to hear? If you were offered one last opportunity to meet with your worst enemy, how would you say what you needed to say in a way that could be heard? What would you need to bring to that meeting that would let you listen to your enemy in a way that they were heard?

Wise and simple speech is one of the hardest of all the branches of mindfulness If silence is perceived as threatening or uncomfortable, we are tempted to fill it with words. In the presence of a dear and trusted friend, the silences that are shared are as significant and treasured as the words that are spoken. In a climate of apprehension or anxiety, words spill from our mouths. We go to a party and find ourselves singing all our old songs, exchanging verbal portfolios with others, endeavoring to impress, or seeking the most distant corner of the room in which to hide. When our hearts and minds are shaken by powerful feelings of anger, hurt, or resentment, our speech seems to take on a momentum and life of its own. We find ourselves speaking words of bitterness where every historical detail of hurt is recounted. When we are most agitated, the pressure of inner unrest seems to unlock our mouths as if the articulation of our every thought is the only way to reclaim inner calm. In all of these moments, awareness appears to be only a distant memory, and mindfulness surrenders before the compelling force of our thoughts, feelings, and words. Often we find ourselves in places far from where we wish to be and we understand that nothing has the power to get us into more trouble than unwise speech. Wise speech is not a destination; it is a practice of simplicity and wisdom.

When my children were growing up they became particularly alert to the moments when they would see me about to deliver a lecture or rebuke they felt to be unfair. As I opened my mouth to launch into a tirade they would turn to me and advise, "Swallow the words." Swallowing the words is wise advice if it guides us to deeper listening and attunement. Clearly it is unwise if it leads us to silence ourselves. Countless people have swallowed the words for too long. People who find themselves inhabiting the shadows of life because of their age, gender, color, or sexuality are familiar with the lethal consequences to their well-being of having swallowed their words and, in doing so, having lost their voice. Dignity in our lives relies upon each of us finding a voice of authenticity that speaks for justice, the end to prejudice and oppression, and the realization of respect. For the disenfranchised and oppressed in our world, the journey of finding their voice takes immense courage and asks from us a receptive, listening silence. Verbal silence can also be used as a weapon of punishment. How many of us have endured silences that are hostile, a withdrawal of love, and an expression of wordless judgment? The discovery of wise speech invites us to find the wisdom both in silence and words. It teaches us to be honest with ourselves and with others, and to speak in a way that fosters dignity, respect, and simplicity.

Wise speech is a careful blend of cultivation and restraint. We cultivate speech that is truthful, helpful, kind, and that leads to harmony and healing. We restrain the words of harshness, divisiveness, and dishonesty that lead to division, mistrust, and the fracturing of our relationships. We listen to the tone of our speech and recognize that in speaking to another we are, in that moment, building a bridge to their heart and that this demands our wholehearted attention. We learn to speak simply, finding the words that make a difference, the words that invite response, and the words that taste of honesty.

Honesty in Speech

Our speech becomes simpler and wiser when we commit ourselves to speaking with truth and honesty. A commitment to integrity needs to be our first loyalty if our speech is to be an expression of respect and dignity. Honesty in our speech inspires trust and confidence from others and invites a reciprocal truthfulness. Yet our understanding of truth needs to be tempered with wisdom. What appears to us to be blatantly true may be an opinion in disguise. We might be tempted to declare, "We live in a materialistic world, empty of meaning." "Gurus are fakes." "Politicians are corrupt." We may find ourselves saying to someone, "You are always defensive, everyone says so," or telling another, "You never listen to me." We may genuinely believe our declarations and statements to be truthful and honest, yet they resemble manifestos more than communication.

Our truth, when imposed upon another person, is rarely received gratefully. Instead it tends to further offence and disconnection and it ignores the fact that no generalization can be absolute. The recipient of our truth may justly feel that they have not been seen in their wholeness, but rather that an image has been created on the basis of one particular aspect of their being. It is also clear that images, generalizations, and opinions that are uttered as absolutes, tend to ignore the reality of impermanence—that what is so obviously true in one moment may be changed in the light of new experience. So, we are startled by a genuine act of honesty and integrity from the politician we dismissed so blithely; a tragedy befalls us and to our surprise we find ourselves being deeply comforted by the silent, devoted presence of the person who "never listens."

Timely Speech

Truth, if it is to be heard, needs to be timely; awareness in our speech embraces both our own commitment to speaking the truth and the context in which it is spoken. Observing a teenage girl mortifying her body so she can resemble the model of the "perfect body" may inspire us to address the truth as we see it. Do we foster a climate of time and space, in which it can be heard in the spirit in which it is intended, rather than as criticism or judgment?

At times, wise speech asks us to say things that are unwelcome or disagreeable to others. It is our responsibility to find the time and the space for these things to be heard. When comforting a bereaved friend we may be tempted to remind them of the changing and fragile nature of all life—it is true, but untimely and probably not the communication that is needed. A friend's house burned down after he left a candle burning. His friends in his spiritual community, with altruistic intentions, reminded him that this was "Surely a test of his practice," "A good time to let go," "A test of his equanimity," and a "Reminder of the need to be mindful." All of this was true, but the communication that was needed was the warmth of a person who truly understood his loss, wept with him, and offered him a home until his house was rebuilt.

Clear Intention

Committing ourselves not only to honesty but also to harmony, we are aware that truth can be a weapon of destruction and alienation when it is used to assert self-righteousness or anger. Our criticism of another may be firmly based in reality and truthfulness, yet our intention is to hurt or punish them. We point out the faults and imperfections in another, convincing ourselves that we are doing it to "help" them. What is the consequence of our truthfulness? Does it lead to a deeper intimacy and trust? Does it foster harmony and understanding? Or does it lead to alienation, distance, and fear? Truthfulness is a precious gift with remarkable powers of transformation, realized in the moments it is communicated, rather than delivered to deafened ears.

We may believe that as long as our intentions are wholesome and good, our words are always justified. With the deepest loving kindness and compassion we point out the flaws and imperfections of another person, but we forget that this person has a heart as filled with fears, anxieties, and wounds as our own. This is a world not always visible to us. We are anxious to correct others, to save them from furthering their shortcomings. Yet intention cannot be the final measure of the wisdom of our speech. We may rebuke another person for their exaggeration, dishonesty, or unkindness, yet their thoughts, feelings, and intentions are not necessarily visible to us. Do we truly understand why they spoke or acted as they did? Can we accept that their inner intentions may be as well motivated as our own? Do we take the time to listen before we speak?

Cultivating wise speech asks us to restrain the inclinations in our hearts and minds that express themselves as unwise speech. It is easy to exaggerate and stretch the truth in order to inflate our own sense of self-importance. It is not always easy to find the wisdom and humility to say, "I don't know," fearing that this will be mistaken for weakness or ineptitude. A Zen master was asked by a devotee what would happen to him after he died. Clearly the student wanted the reassurance and comfort of certainty, and was shocked when his teacher answered, "I don't know." Indignant, the student rebuked him, "You are supposed to be so wise, such a knowledgeable Buddhist, how can you not know the answer to this most important of all questions?" His teacher answered, "Probably because I am not a dead Buddhist."

Cultivating Truthfulness

Culturally we are not always encouraged in the pathways of truthfulness. How many industries and professions rely upon something less than honesty? We are promised that a potion will defy aging, that there is a remedy for all pain, and that a hair transplant will make us loveable. We may hear that a particular strategy or possession will guarantee success and admiration, or that a certain spiritual technique will guarantee happiness or liberation. One woman spoke to me of her decision to change her profession after becoming increasingly aware that her success relied upon her ability to convince people that they needed things that would not bring them lasting happiness, but instead only feelings of avarice and deprivation.

As we learn to speak more truthfully, we discover that being mindful of our speech is a key to becoming aware of our inner life and the quality of our relationships. Out of our commitment to honesty we discover the voice to speak for justice, compassion, and integrity. We worry less about the applause that may follow our words, are less interested in the approval and affirmation of others, and treasure integrity and compassion more than popularity. The honesty reflected in our speech leaves few residues of regret or guilt in our minds. We are increasingly willing to take responsibility for the anger and fear that arises in our hearts, rather than disguising them in opinions or judgment. The peace we discover in an unclouded heart and mind is manifested in our speech, and in the growing peace and confidence in our relationships with others.

In cultivating a voice rooted in wisdom and simplicity we learn to restrain speech that is harsh or abusive, and to cultivate kindness, sensitivity, and respect in our words. Anger is a powerful emotional energy that constantly seeks an outlet. The tension that surrounds anger is sometimes so volatile and unendurable that catharsis appears to offer the only relief. Accusations and abuse directed at another become a means of relieving ourselves of the pain of our own anger. We insist on being heard, on making our point, yet in doing so we create an even deeper pain—the pain of separation and division. Our words can never be taken back and they can leave a residue of pain and fear in the heart of another. Suppressed anger creates pain in the obsessive inner preoccupation with words that have not been said. It takes remarkable patience and compassion to find the willingness to pause before words of anger are hurled at another. At times this pause is born of the wisdom that recognizes that the only point we make in the impulsive expression of anger is that we may be a person to fear and avoid. In finding the willingness to pause and listen to ourselves before we speak, we may also discover the confidence and calmness to speak with a firmness and clarity that can be heard. Kindness and compassion do not always mean that we say "Yes." There are countless views, actions, and beliefs in our world, that are unacceptable because of the harm, suffering, and alienation they breed. The awakening energy asks us to say "No" and to find the words and actions of healing within ourselves. Healing, reconciliation, and understanding are unlikely to be born of abuse. With understanding and compassion we can learn to channel angry passion into a voice that contributes to uprooting injustice.

A climate of scorn, blame, harshness, or rage is not an environment in which we find the trust or safety to listen, open our hearts, or receive another. Faced with insults, sarcasm, or accusation, our first response is to protect ourselves, avoid our abuser, or respond with equal aggression. Engaging in harsh, abusive, or sarcastic speech, we do not invite another person to trust or listen to what we are trying to say. Anger and abuse have the power to divide people from one another. Hatred grows from the seeds of abusive speech and we become both victims and perpetrators of division.

Cultivating kindness, sensitivity, and gentleness in our speech is a direct result of cultivating patience, tolerance, and respect in our hearts. Cultivating mindfulness, care, and simplicity in our speech becomes a means of reminding ourselves that we live as part of an indivisible organism whose harmony relies upon each of us living and speaking with kindness and compassion. We discover that a person deeply embedded in integrity and inner confidence has little need to shout their truths. Their silence speaks as loudly as their words.

Words of Meaning

Cultivating a voice of wisdom and simplicity, we gladly refrain from useless, idle speech and instead speak words that are meaningful and conducive to clarity. We seek to bridge the pain of distance, alienation, and loneliness through our words. We reach out to another through our speech, asking to be acknowledged, seen, and connected. A young, homeless man stands on a street corner in Berkeley, shouting, "I exist, I am alive!" Many of our words seem to hold no meaning; they carry within them this deeper need to be visible and acknowledged by others. Not knowing how to touch the heart of another and forge loving, meaningful connections, we speak words that leave us frustrated and isolated. We speak so many words to comfort ourselves, to reassure ourselves that we are not alone, yet they leave behind them a vacuum of unfulfilled loving. Feeling isolated, we drown ourselves in the idle chatter of radios, muzac, and background noise, but this does little to ease loneliness; instead it serves to agitate our own minds and hearts. Within all the complexity born of the agitated mind, we find little space to listen inwardly or outwardly, to find the words that communicate meaning.

Refraining from idle chatter is a practice of mindfulness that cultivates simplicity. Before we open our mouths we learn to pause and listen to ourselves. Pai-Chang advised, "Close your lips, and say something." What is it we truly wish to say? Is it helpful and needed? If we bring to our encounters with others a wholehearted attention, we discover that this simple, heartfelt presence weighs more than a thousand squandered words. To listen before we speak is the heart of wise and simple communication. Words that are born of deep listening are a treasure, communicating meaning, and they leave behind them a residue of love. They have a taste of freedom.

Gossip

Treasuring simplicity, healing, and awareness we learn to refrain from gossip. Recently, I read a theory that one of the benefits of having an enemy is that it brings you closer to others through shared aversion and judgment. How reassured we can feel in our dislike of a person when it is confirmed through gossip? In gossip we rarely highlight the positive, wholesome, or loving qualities of another person. What are accentuated are the perceived shortcomings, flaws, and imperfections of others. The more we speak of those flaws, repeat them, and expand upon them, the more the degree of solidity they assume increases. Reciting another person's perceived flaws opens the door to aversion. We remember the countless ways our enemy has been offensive in the past and the words they have spoken suddenly assume a darker significance. Our enemy is exiled from our hearts.

Our enemy becomes stereotyped through gossip, and a mythology founded on aversion or fear is imposed on them. The greatest unkindness inherent in stereotyping is that it freezes a person in an image or myth that does not allow space for them to change. Through gossip we banish the totality of another person from our heart; we discredit and silence them. The cruelty of gossip is that it deprives our enemy of the opportunity to be understood, to change, and to be listened to. Gossip is the infliction of suffering from a distance that appears to protect us. Yet we are not protected. Our hearts know that we carry residues of gossip with us long after a conversation has ended. Inwardly, we know we have sacrificed sensitivity, kindness, and compassion, and we are left with the bitterness of that surrender.

Treasuring in our hearts a commitment to intimacy, understanding, and compassion, we surrender gossip rather than wisdom. We learn to find the words that lead to harmony rather than division, that are peaceful rather than harsh, that have a taste of freedom rather than delusion. Our speech becomes much simpler, calmer, and more worthy. We find the words that lead toward happiness, that earn the trust and respect of another, and that foster loving kindness.

Learning to Listen

Wise speech is founded upon our capacity to listen whole-heartedly. To listen well we are asked to learn to be more empty, to lay down the complexity of our expectations, opinions, chatter, and the agitation that clouds our minds. A Japanese master received a university professor who came to ask about Zen. The professor introduced himself with a long list of his qualifications and successes that portrayed his brilliance, and then he pulled out a long list of questions about the meaning of life and the path of Zen. The master picked up the teapot, filled his visitor's cup, and then, much to the professor's astonishment, continued pouring. The professor watched the tea spill over and begin to run off the table onto the floor. Unable to restrain himself any longer, he blurted, "The cup is over full. No more will go in!" "This cup is like your own mind," the master said. "How can I show you Zen unless you first empty your cup?"

The power of silence is that it teaches us to listen. Listening wholeheartedly to another we receive not only their words, but also the world of feeling, emotion, and intention that lies beneath the words. We learn to respond to the whole of another person, not just to the words that are spoken. Loving, receptive silence invites the confidence and trust of others. Learning to listen inwardly, we learn to pause before assuming any of our conclusions or opinions are absolute truths. We listen to the deeper world of our hearts and minds, too often hidden by the torrent of our words. Words born of silence are words of peace and meaning, compassion and care that span the abyss which separates us from another. Wise speech is the greatest of all arts, learned in the classroom of silence. In that moment when story and judgment do not interfere, we discover the rich silence of listening in which heartfelt connection is discovered.

GUIDED MEDITATION

Imagine finding yourself alone in a room with a person whom you have long struggled with or have been hurt by.

What would you need to bring to the encounter that would enable you to be heard and understood? What words would you need to find that would communicate not just the songs of history, but also the pain of the moment? How would you need to say those words so they could be listened to? What would you need to let go of in your own heart so that you could listen to them?

Imagine yourself in the same room with a dear friend about to leave on a journey that has no end. What words would you want to offer to them that they could take with them? How would you speak and how would you listen?

When you leave your home in the morning to go out into the world, experiment by going with a committed intention to speak only what is truthful, helpful, and sensitive, just for one day. Attune yourself through your day to the words you speak and how you listen. What difference does it make?

Speaking honestly needs to be linked to a heart of kindness and compassion. Our words shouted in anger and accusation may be truthful in their message, but they will mostly fall on deaf ears. Anger makes people afraid and closed. When our anger speaks more loudly than the truth, it is the anger that is heard.

CHAPTER

9

mindfulness

The whole world is a door of liberation, inviting us to enter.

ZEN

EXPERIENCING a deep hunger for liberation, the young prince Siddhartha left behind his palace of ease and pleasure, and set out on a journey. Believing the world to be a prison, Siddhartha heroically attempted to escape from his body, heart, mind, and world. Through depriving himself of food he mortified his body until his skeleton was visible through his skin. Disdaining his mind, he endeavored to force it into submission through concentration and will. Trying to transcend his heart, he divorced himself from human contact, living in seclusion and avoiding all engagement with the world. He discovered that he

164

could not bypass himself on the way to enlightenment, that life would simply not go away. While frail, weak, and near death from starvation, a woman came to him and offered him a bowl of food. It was a simple gesture that returned Siddhartha to himself. Receptive to the care and compassion expressed in that offering, a similar response of care and compassion was evoked in Siddhartha's heart. Taking care of his body with compassion, he returned to this world of sounds, sights, touch, and feelings, with a renewed appreciation and understanding. He acknowledged that if liberation were to be found, it would be found in the midst of this very life.

This was the beginning of the "middle" path. He discovered the path of mindfulness, learning that the key to freedom was offered in each breath, step, thought, feeling, sound, and sight. Caught in the struggle of "good" and "bad," "sacred" and "worldly," "spiritual" and "mundane," he became lost in the eternal struggle of the mind of being "for" and "against," In that struggle he sought enlightenment everywhere but where he was, and he experienced the frustration of being shadowed by the world he sought to transcend. Siddhartha began to understand that it was not the world that he needed to transcend, but the clouds of misunderstanding that imprisoned his mind. With this change of heart came the understanding that there was no better moment in which to awaken than in the present moment. Everything offered in that present moment, in his body, mind, and heart, held the possibility of deepening the sensitivity, wisdom, and compassion that he had desperately sought elsewhere. Freedom, he understood, did not depend on departing from the world, but on turning toward this world and this moment with mindfulness. A much later sage advised, "The best way to make our dreams come true is for us to wake up."

The "middle" path lies at the heart of the teaching of awakening. Mindfulness is the means and the end, the path and the destination. It is the ultimate path of simplicity. Mindfulness is as relevant to a nun cloistered in a mountain cave as to an executive in a boardroom. To cultivate the art of mindfulness, we do not have to belong to a particular religion, have a long spiritual portfolio, or learn a new vocabulary or set of rituals. Wherever and whenever we are, is the perfect place and time to be mindful, to engage wholeheartedly with the moment, and to be taught by it. It is a "nothing special" practice in which each moment and encounter becomes "special" through the mindfulness that illuminates it.

The Richness of Mindfulness

Mindfulness is not only a technique or practice, but is concerned with the quality of wakeful presence and the willingness to learn that we bring to each moment in our lives. It is saturated with sensitivity and curiosity, with the willingness to make peace with all moments and all things, and the deep wish to be free wherever we are. Mindfulness illuminates all things and all activities. It encourages engagement and participation in each moment, and brings profound understanding and awakening. It is deeper than a passing experience, but it embraces all experiences without prejudice, finding balance and steadiness in the extremes of our lives.

Mindfulness is no stranger to us. The richest, deepest moments of our lives have all been moments of mindfulness—the moments in our childhood when our hearts sang with delight over the simple arrangement of the pebbles on the path, the moments when we have stood speechless before the majesty of a forest, the moments we have rejoiced in a sunset, the moments when we have been a silent, listening presence with a friend in pain. The times in our lives when we have turned toward pain in our bodies or minds with the willingness to understand, the times when we have appreciated the moments of ecstasy and pleasure yet also understood their transience—these too are moments of mindfulness. In the complexity of our lives we forget the power of these moments, yet their memory lingers, reminding us of the depth of peace and freedom possible. We know that we cannot maintain these moments of richness and each time we try to prevent their passing they are already lost. We come to understand that mindfulness, presence, and wakefulness are ways of being to be rediscovered in each moment. Mindfulness is neither difficult nor complex; *remembering* to be mindful is the great challenge.

Mindfulness has been called the art of recollection, of remembering ourselves—where we are and how we are. Perhaps this seems simplistic, yet we only need to examine a single day in our lives to appreciate the power of forgetfulness. We can live a life of countless "lost" moments. Leaning back into the past or forward into the future, we forget where we are. Lost in the addictive power of our thoughts, daydreams, and fantasies we forget to listen, to see, and to touch. Lost in the events of the world, in our anticipations and fears, we forget the life of our bodies. Lost in our words, we forget to listen. This world of forgetting is the inner and outer world of complexity that suffocates simplicity and sensitivity. Mindfulness rescues us from a forgotten life, teaches us to be present and engaged, concerned less with what is happening and more with how we are present in all moments. We learn to recollect ourselves, to gather our attention and bring a wholehearted presence to each moment. Mindfulness is a shortcut to happiness.

Cultivating Oneness

The cultivation of oneness is both the path and the destination of mindfulness. Through remembering to bring a whole-hearted attention to each moment, we integrate our body, mind, heart, and the moment we are in. We listen to a piece of music, the words of another person, or even to the sound of traffic outside our window, and the sounds ripple through our whole body, mind, and heart—the attention and presence we bring leaps across the gap that often seems to separate us from where we are. We open a door and feel the touch of our fingers on the wood, we feel the ground beneath our feet, the breeze on our face and this single step becomes a miracle of attention. Our body twinges with pain or responds to the warmth of a caring touch and we receive both with sensitivity, exploring our responses, and honoring that moment of feeling with wholehearted attention. A wise woman once remarked, "I have adopted the practice of living from miracle to miracle."

Mindfulness is a powerful antidote to the fragmentation that governs our lives. Standing on a hilltop overlooking a beautiful valley, we find ourselves worrying about whether we brought enough sandwiches, or about a meeting scheduled for the next day. A child pleads for our attention, but our attention is already battling with the busyness of a day yet to be experienced. Our body asks for our attention, but we tell ourselves we have no time to listen. These moments of fragmentation are not difficult to heal, but they are moments that plead for our heartfelt attention.

The cultivation of oneness is the cultivation of peace; the cultivation of mindfulness teaches us to engage fully with the moment we are in. We pay the price of fragmentation in stress, disconnection, and depression. Learning to treasure each moment, we learn to live in a sacred way, honoring each single moment. Bowing is a frequently cultivated ritual in the Zen tradition. Students bow to the teacher, to each other, to their food, and to their meditation cushion. They bow to the monastery dogs, to the passing garbage trucks, to the daily tasks of cleaning and cooking. Mindfulness is a symbolic bow to each moment, reminding us not to stand outside our lives but within them. Each time we bow to life, we dissolve separation and discover the peace of oneness.

Mindfulness is the direct experience of the simple truths of each moment. We might call this "pre-verbal"—a way of seeing and embracing each moment undistorted by our descriptions, values, preferences, or stories. Learning to see things just as they are is the renunciation of all the arguments we have with the world. Our likes and dislikes, "shoulds" and judgments interfere powerfully with our capacity to find peace with all the moments and encounters of our lives. Like a radio not quite in tune, our capacity to see clearly is clouded by the noise we superimpose upon the moment. We spend so much time trying to fix the world, ourselves, our experience, and other people so we can remain undisturbed. Mindfulness does not deny wise and skillful action, but it knows that true freedom is not born of "fixing", but of understanding.

The Intimacy of Mindfulness

With wholehearted attention we find a growing intimacy and closeness with each arising and passing moment. We learn to argue less, just to be with what is. Mindfulness has the flavor of calm receptivity; it reminds us of that powerful moment of presence before the words begin to flow. On the periphery of our vision we catch sight of our face reflected in the mirror. In that moment before the arguments begin about what we see, declaiming the bags under our eyes, the appearance of a new wrinkle, or the mess of our hair, we have a glimpse of pure mindfulness. It is a moment of just seeing, still, calm, and receptive. Describing the simplicity of mindfulness, the Buddha encouraged, "In the seeing there is just the seeing. In the hearing there is just the hearing. In the walking just the walking."

Mindfulness reminds us of the freedom and wisdom to be found in each moment. Arguing less with the world, we discover what each moment has to say to us. Mindfulness brings with it a receptivity that allows the world to tell its story. Some years ago I was invited to teach a retreat in the desert in Arizona. Countless people had spoken to me about the beauty and magnificence of the desert, and I was eager to experience it for myself. Arriving late in the night I was impatient for morning to come so I could catch my first glimpse of the desert. Setting my alarm so I could experience the sunrise, I was outside, ready and waiting at first light for this experience to unfold. As the sun rose, I looked around and a single disappointed thought arose, "It's brown." The story soon followed, "What is so beautiful about brown? It all looks the same—flat, lifeless, and uninspiring. These people, with their stories, must have been in a different desert." Slightly disheartened, I went on to teach a retreat. Over the days I found time to walk in the desert and I discovered that the more I looked, listened, and felt, the more I saw. The desert was teeming with life. The heat haze shimmered over the ground. Within the brown there were countless subtle shades and textures. Each hour as the sun moved, casting different shadows and light, the desert was changed. It was a wondrous, alive, shifting, changing reality, different in each moment of the day.

For anything in this world to be alive for us, we are asked to be alive to it. Mindfulness awakens not only our way of seeing, but also everything that is seen. If we look carefully at anything that we take for granted, we understand that it is the power of mindfulness which allows us to see it with new eyes, to be taught by it. It is only our concepts and images that stay the same, not our lives. The words and concepts are pale shadows of reality. Treasuring the richness of direct experience we learn to attend closely to the sights, sounds, touches, and activities we encounter, discovering the moment before the stories begin. We begin to discover that our stories are far less satisfying than the direct connection with reality.

Unconditional Welcome

Mindfulness has a flavor; it is not passive, resigned, or static, but alive, vital, receptive, and responsive. Within mindfulness there is a quality of wise acceptance and welcome. We tend to describe many of the events, circumstances, people, or inner experiences in our lives as obstacles that inhibit freedom and peace. We try to flee from them, avoid or alter them. We see ourselves, with our body, mind, history, or heart, as an obstacle to freedom. The things in our life we call obstacles are mostly the experiences we find ourselves unable or unwilling to welcome. Mindfulness is being intimate with all things, including those we fear or hate the most. As we find the willingness within ourselves to turn our attention towards those things we most fear or dislike, we discover that one of the great mysteries of mindfulness is its power to turn our enemies into allies. The most direct path to transformation and wisdom is to turn our attention towards whatever we most deeply wish to flee from. In doing so we release ourselves from disconnection, fear, and powerlessness.

The quality of mindfulness is not a neutral or blank presence. True mindfulness is imbued with warmth, compassion, and interest. In the light of this engaged attention we discover it is impossible to hate or fear anything or anyone that we truly understand. The nature of mindfulness is engagement; where there is interest, a natural, unforced attention follows.

Mindfulness is a present moment experience, concerned with embracing and understanding the entirety of each moment. This is not a denial of past or future, but an understanding that both past and future arise in the present through our thoughts. Memory carries within it volumes of past experiences with all their joys and sorrows. In reality they have gone by, never to be repeated and beyond alteration, yet they are given life in the present through thought. Plans, rehearsals, anticipations, and decisions about a time that has yet to happen appear in our mind. Mindfulness does not attempt to erase the past or deny the future, but is concerned with now. In truth, we don't get lost in the past or the future, we get lost in our thoughts about them. The simplicity of mindfulness is that it teaches us not to be lost in our stories, but to use our capacity to see thought as thought, as part of an interwoven tapestry of the present. We learn to take our seat in the moment and treasure it as the home of transformation. Mindfulness embraces every particular of our life yet seizes upon none of them. The sounds, sights, tastes, touches, thoughts, and feelings we experience are the story of each moment embraced in mindfulness. Listening deeply, taking hold of nothing, mindfulness teaches us the story of freedom.

The Buddha described this quality of vast unshakeable presence as the heart of freedom, saying:

Don't revive the past,
Or on the future build your hopes.
The past has been left behind
And the future is yet to come.
Instead with understanding see,
Each presently arisen moment
Invincibly, unshakably.
Today is the day this effort can be made
Tomorrow, death may come, who knows?
No bargain with mortality can death defy
But a person who resides fully present and awake
By day and by night
They are the peaceful sage.

Mindfulness is a consciousness free of all preference and prejudice. It is vast, alive, welcoming, and poised. It can be likened to a mirror that reflects all things without distinction and that detects the wisdom they carry. The mirror doesn't choose to see only the beautiful, rejecting the unpleasant. It doesn't struggle to hold onto one image or prevent a less favorable one from arising. Everything that appears in that mirror holds its own seed of wisdom, inviting participation and understanding. Milarepa, a great master, once said, "Even a wandering thought is the essence of wisdom." Mindfulness awakens our capacity to glean understanding and compassion from everything our world presents.

Over time different traditions and disciplines have sought to formulate paths, practices, and techniques that draw us closer to an understanding of the freedom found within each mindfully lived moment. These practices are reflections of mindfulness, just as the image of the sun reflected on a pond is a reflection of the sun itself. They show us a way of intimacy and engagement bringing us closer to the simple truths of each moment, and they teach us how to let go, simplify, and bring a quality of reverence to each moment in our lives. The essence of all these paths and practices is the cultivation of bare attention and clear understanding. These are the two powerful truths which encourage us to penetrate to the heart of each moment and the heart of freedom.

Bare Attention

What is bare attention? It is the willingness and capacity to bring a wholehearted attention to each moment without adding anything to it, without trying to detract from it, alter it, or layer it with interpretation. With bare attention there is no sense of ownership brought to the moment; it is not "my" experience, not happening to "me," nor am "I" making it happen. It is just happening. We walk outdoors and stub our toe on a stone. The simple truth of that moment is the toe and the stone, the meeting and the sensation. The complex story of that moment is "My toe," "Which fool put that stone there?"' "Why do these things always happen to me?" "Every stone is an enemy," and "Every step we take is fraught with disaster."

The moment we move from the simple truth to the complex history, we enter a world of struggle, fear, confusion, and complexity. Each time we return to the simple truth we rediscover peace, calmness, and simplicity. Compelled by the complex story and the words we use to scold or reassure ourselves, or blame the world, we may tempted to hurl insults at both the stone and our toe and go into our day carrying with us the frustration of our misadventure. Resting in the simple truth of the moment we might carefully move the stone to a less hazardous spot, bandage our toe, and move into our day leaving that encounter in its place.

Bare attention is cultivated in each moment without exception. The thought is just the thought, the sound the sound, the taste the taste, the feeling the feeling. There is no judgment or prejudice within this wholehearted attention—the pleasant and unpleasant are equally embraced, the challenging and the easy, the flattering and the unflattering. A life without judgment is a free life, an engaged, steady, receptive presence in the presence of all things. The countless burdens of history, projection, association, and fear are laid down. Through the encompassing nature of bare attention, we live in a world where we have no enemies, but instead an ongoing invitation to learn, to listen, and to understand.

Calmness is the fruit of bare attention. The mind is released from its agitation and preoccupation, free to see more deeply and simply. The world itself seems to calm down when it is no longer perceived as a combative arena. In deeper levels of attention the mind and body come to depths of calmness that are in themselves joyful, still, and radiant. Attention is our bridge to the simple truths of the moment. A Zen master was asked about the key to happiness. Reflecting for a moment he answered with a single word: "Attention."

The quality of transforming attention is one of curiosity and interest. Burglars may have wonderful concentration, a soldier going into battle may be remarkably focused, and a stalker may have a highly developed single-pointedness. But there is a real difference between the concentration of obsession and pre-occupation, and the attention of mindfulness. Mindful attention is light, gentle, warm; above all it is dedicated to understanding and freedom. It is both single pointed, and open and receptive in the same moment. The quality of bare attention can be likened to that of a mother cradling her child. Held too tightly the infant will complain; held too loosely and there will be unfortunate consequences. Gentle, devoted, caring attention embraces the moment.

Dissolving Habit

The greatest barriers to mindful attention lie in the territory of habit and in the addiction to pleasant sensation. Habit prevents us from perceiving the richness and learning offered in each moment. The adage that "familiarity breeds contempt" has particular significance in the development of mindfulness. The habits of our actions, thoughts, responses, and lives veil our capacity to see with depth. Habit is a pattern of dismissive-ness—we deem whatever we do habitually to be unworthy of our attention. In the withdrawal of our attention we deprive ourselves of the capacity to be touched, to see each moment anew, and to be taught by the lessons of the moment. When we are lost in habit—washing the dishes we have washed a thousand times before—we fantasize about the perfect moment that lies in the future. Greeting our partner as we have done countless times before, our attention is elsewhere and we fail to see them. Responding to ourselves with familiar and habitual patterns of judgment, blame, or aversion, we imprison ourselves in a history. Habit is a surrender of sensitivity; mindful attention is reclaiming sensitivity so that the moment is transformed.

It makes a wonderful difference to our lives to bring wholehearted attention to moments, actions, and responses that are shrouded in habit. We can drive our car as if it was the most important journey of our lives. We can play with our child as if it was to be our last encounter with them. We can listen to ourselves as if we were listening to a Buddha. These become powerful moments and teachers through simple depth of attention.

Addiction to Pleasure

The other great obstacle to mindful attention is our addiction to pleasure; an addiction that holds within it our fear of being overwhelmed or paralyzed by the unpleasant, challenging thoughts, encounters, feelings, and sensations that are part of the fabric of our lives. By filling our senses and minds with food, sound, information, and entertainment, we also numb ourselves. Increasingly, we find it difficult to embrace the unpleasant events or challenges that life brings us. We forget the simple truth that freedom relies upon embracing the whole of our life and world. Busy with pursuing, avoiding, and modifying we attempt to convince ourselves that we are safe from the unpredictability of a life that offers no guarantees. We try to build sandcastles before an oncoming tide.

Our life will continue to bring us the sweet, delightful, even glorious moments, but it will also bring the sour. We cannot command the world or our mind to deliver to us only the pleasant and shield us from the unpleasant. Bare attention teaches us to find balance and steadiness; it protects us from fear and offers a reliable refuge in a changing and fragile world. Mindfulness is always available and we are invited to help ourselves to the peace and freedom it offers.

The stillness and calmness born of bare attention are not ends in themselves but a door to liberating wisdom. They are the foundation upon which understanding is built. Wisdom is an understanding of the nature of life and of ourselves, deeply seeing what is true on a cellular level. Listening to the story of the present moment invites us to understand the story of all moments.

The Changing Seasons of the Moment

Stand still in the forest in autumn and let the trees tell you their story. The vibrantly colored leaves falling from the branches speak to us of the seasons of life. Birth, aging, sickness, and death—all the seasons of change are held within the falling of a single leaf. The leaf on the ground becomes part of the loam that allows new seeds to grow. The leaf is not separate from the tree but is born of the tree; it is also not exactly the same as the tree. Intimations of change are held in each passing moment and there is nothing in this life exempt from that rhythm. We are taught by those intimations; to try to interfere with a passing season is to enter into conflict, struggle, and sorrow. There is a freedom in absorbing the simple truth of change—to live in harmony with this understanding is to find peace in all the changes of our lives.

Seeing the changing seasons we understand the way to the end of separation, conflict, and confusion. We learn to let go, to let be. We stand amid the perpetually changing seasons of each moment. Everything that is born will die; everything that arises will pass away. Nothing is exempt. Whenever we endeavor to separate ourselves from this rhythm we create a world of struggle and fear. Each time we cling to or grasp any thought, experience, feeling, or encounter embraced in the rhythm of change, we set ourselves apart from the world. Mindfulness is the art of non-interference, of not clinging anywhere. In not dwelling anywhere, not fixating upon anything, we are present everywhere. In not clinging to anything, we are not defined by anything and our freedom is limitless. The Buddha remarked, "The mind that does not cling, does not become agitated. The mind that is not agitated is close to freedom."

Standing in the forest amid its life we come to see that no one is making all this happen. The buds form on the branches, the sun, the rain, and the richness of the soil provide the conditions for those buds to develop into leaves. The heat of the summer, the winds of autumn, and the first frosts of winter all affect the life of a single leaf, which will eventually fade and fall. Everything is interdependent. Life interacts with itself. If the conditions changed, if there was a drought or the tree was damaged, a different process would simply occur. The conditions of life are constantly changing and perpetually affecting and influencing our experience of each moment. We are not always in control of these conditions and our commands are mostly futile, but we are not powerless. The seeds of peace lie within the mindful presence brought to each moment.

The life of the forest is a reflection of our own life. Within our body, mind, and heart, we experience the process of change in every moment. Thoughts, feelings, bodily sensations, and experiences all arise and pass away. Our world of this moment is affected and formed by where we are, what we are exposed to, and how we meet the simple truths of each moment. It is futile to believe that at the center of this unfolding and interacting process there is a controlling entity. As we learn to be intimate with ourselves and all things, we understand that nothing and no one is separate from the changing conditions of the moment. Our understanding and sense of who we are undergoes countless changes in a single day. The angry "me" changes into the "me" of tolerance and patience. The hopeful, excited "self" of the afternoon has quite forgotten the "self" that brooded and obsessed over breakfast. We begin to discover that it is impossible to find any sense of "self" apart from our beliefs.

The deep, transforming understanding of change, suffering and its cause, and the end of suffering, is the wisdom of mindfulness. The secret of the Buddha's smile is endlessly speculated upon. Perhaps he smiled at himself for spending years searching outside of himself for the freedom that was always in his heart. Mindfulness is born in each moment we turn our attention to where we are. With gentle, calm attention we engage with this moment; probing beneath the surface to understand the simple truth of the moment, we are taught by it. Freedom is not complicated or distant. We are asked to be present. Suzuki Roshi, a wise teacher, reminded us, "To a sincere student, every day is a fortunate day."

GUIDED MEDITATION

Choose any action in your day that is taken for granted—walking up the stairs, driving the car, answering the telephone. Bring to that activity the clear intention to attend closely to all its details—listen to your body, be sensitive to the quality of your mind, be wholeheartedly with it. Sense what a difference it makes.

Take a few moments in your day to listen wholeheartedly. Be aware of how you receive the sounds that come to you. Listen to the silence between the sounds. Explore what it means to bring a heartfelt attention to your body, your mind, or a single emotion. Sense the simple truths that lie beneath the concepts, prejudices, and labels. Ask yourself,

■ "Where is peace? Where is freedom?"

awakening

Enlightenment is like the moon reflected on the water.

The moon does not get wet, nor is the water broken.

Although its light is wide and great,

The moon is reflected even in a puddle an inch wide.

The whole moon and the entire sky are reflected

in one dewdrop on the grass.

DOGEN

THE young prince Siddhartha lived an idyllic life in the palace under the watchful eyes of his parents. Desiring that his son would never stray from his destiny to be king, his father showered the prince with every conceivable pleasure, comfort, and delight. Beautiful sights and sounds, entertainment and distraction filled his days and nights. Even the wilting flowers and leaves in the royal gardens were removed so that Siddhartha would never see a single thing to disturb his mind. His life was filled with the young, the beautiful, and the pleasing. The king made every effort to provide a life so enticing and entrancing that Siddhartha would never want to leave.

As a young man Siddhartha decided he wanted to see more of the city that surrounded the palace. Unable to refuse his son anything, the king issued orders decreeing that any sight that might possibly disturb the royal prince be removed from the city. The streets were swept, the houses painted, flowers strewn along the road Siddhartha would travel, and only the young and beautiful inhabitants of the city were invited to view the royal procession. As the prince went out in his chariot and greeted his well-wishers, he spotted an elderly man, bowed with age, his face wrinkled with years. Shocked, Siddhartha turned to his driver and asked, "What is this?" His driver answered, "This is old age." Bemused, Siddhartha returned to the palace. Over the following days he made further trips into the city, one day seeing a young woman desperately ill, wracked with pain; on another seeing a corpse being brought from a house, surrounded by mourning relatives. Each time Siddhartha asked his driver to explain what he was seeing. "Illness and death," he was told. Siddhartha would ask, "Will this also happen to me?" and he was assured that it would. On the last of his ventures into the city, Siddhartha saw in the crowd a wandering holy man, simply and poorly dressed, yet with radiance and serenity etched upon his face. On asking for an explanation he was told this was a man dedicated to living a sacred life.

Returning to the palace, Siddhartha found himself unable to rest. The images that had made such a profound impact upon him kept running through his mind. Soon afterwards, shaken and disturbed, Siddhartha left his palace and his life, to begin his own search for an enduring peace, happiness, and freedom. The meeting with aging, sickness, death, and renunciation—the four heavenly messengers—was a profound turning point in Siddhartha's life, a moment of awakening. It was not only a life of certainty and ease in the royal palace that he left behind, but more significantly, the palace of his illusions.

The meeting with the heavenly messengers penetrated his world-view of life being controllable and answerable to his desires, that fleeting pleasures were equal to happiness, and that immortality was possible. His illusions were shattered by the direct encounter with aging, sickness, and death, and so his life was changed. The loss of his illusions did not lead to disappointment, despair, or rage, but instead awakened in Siddhartha a spark of divine curiosity, a mature dissatisfaction with his life, and a thirst for freedom. Fundamental questions were awakened in Siddhartha's heart through his meeting with the heavenly messengers. What was the meaning of his life, his place in the world? Where could true refuge and peace be found? The deepest question—who he was apart from his role, his identity, his history, and his culture—lingered in his heart.

The Palace of Illusions

In those pivotal meetings, Siddhartha understood that his palace of delight was actually a prison in which the jailers were well hidden. He was sublimely comfortable and protected in his illusions, but he was not free. His palace was a fragile structure, sustained by and dependent upon the denial of reality. Siddhartha was startled into wakefulness through the intrusion of reality, and so began a journey on which there were no sure voices to guide him and no assurances of success. Suspicious of the past and uncertain of the future, Siddhartha could only heed an awakened inner voice that treasured freedom above all else. Going from a life of total self-indulgence to a life of total self-denial and finding freedom in neither, Siddhartha had no choice but to stop, take his seat beneath the Bodhi tree, and open his heart to the wisdom offered in each moment.

Our own illusions are constantly challenged by reality, and we are startled into wakefulness. Loss, death, failure, and separation touch all of our lives and they directly expose us to the uncertainty and fragility of everything we rely upon. Our bodies are not exempt from aging, nor from sickness, but they are a testimony to the process of change that underlies all life. The heavenly messengers are never far from us. We meet the beggar on the street and feelings of compassion and irritation arise. We pick up a newspaper and digest the reality of the violence, pain, and fear that are the daily diet of countless people. We also meet the powerful symbols of compassion, love, patience, and courage that invite us to awaken.

The intrusion of reality asks each of us to leave behind our palaces of illusion, whether they are illusions of certainty, permanence, safety, control, or identity. When our world-views are shattered, sometimes we leave our palaces gracefully and sometimes we are evicted from them. All moments when our illusions fall away are moments of awakening, turning points that invite us to embrace the reality of this moment gracefully.

The Tension of Awakening

There is an inevitable tension in any journey of awakening. There may be reluctance to leave our palaces behind, even when we understand they may be prisons. They have been comfortable prisons to us. To awaken to new realities demands great courage, faith, perseverance, and patience, and we are not sure we have enough of these qualities. Yet we know we cannot turn back from moments of awakening; we cannot reclaim a world that has changed beyond recognition or a "self" that has been altered by experience. There is little choice but to face a future that is unknown to us and to learn to trust in the present. The shattering of any illusion invites a change of heart, and the changes we go through are an invitation for everyone around us to change. Awakening is sometimes a painful process. We begin to understand that the seed of freedom is planted in the soil of great need and sorrow.

Experience alone does not hold an intrinsic power to awaken us; it is our capacity to learn from experience that does this. Siddhartha could have returned to the palace and submerged the impact of the heavenly messengers beneath an ocean of distraction. Each day we are impacted by moments of confusion, pain, loss, sorrow, and change, but they do not intrinsically change us. If experience alone were at the heart of awakening we would live in an enlightened world. What does death teach us? What do loss and change teach us? What do disappointment, failure, sickness, and sorrow teach us? Do we turn towards the heavenly messengers and say, "Welcome" or do we turn away and ignore their message? The central teaching of the heavenly messengers is "Let go," "Rely upon nothing," "Cling to nothing," and "Discover what it means to be free."

A group of researchers investigating spiritual experience were surprised to discover that of the hundreds of people they interviewed, 82% claimed to have had a mystical experience at some point in their lives. Of these, 90% said that they never wanted to have another one. We often walk a tightrope between our wish to escape from the world, save it, or immerse ourselves in it. There exist within us two polarized forces. A genuine thirst for authenticity, awakening, and freedom, is accompanied by an equally powerful desire to remain undisturbed. The truth is that life disturbs us, because it is rarely obedient to our wishes and it will not stand still for us. Meditative paths are dedicated to the cultivation of peace and serenity, but they are also intended to disturb us deeply—to challenge all of our illusions and beliefs in the quest for awakening. Ralph Waldo Emerson remarked, "People wish to be settled; only so far as they are unsettled is there any hope for them."

The "holy" fools and masters in many spiritual traditions are teachers of disturbance, never allowing their students to cling to anything. A young Western student practiced heroically in a Japanese monastery, "sweating beads." Sleep-deprived, hungry, and lonely, he felt himself to be on the verge of a nervous breakdown. Prostrating himself before the roshi, he burst into tears and confessed he was ready to give up. To his amazement the roshi burst into laughter and exclaimed, "You've done it, this is satori." Announcements were made in the monastery, the local television station came to film the "awakened" Westerner and he was the recipient of congratulation and praise from all. After some days, basking in his new "awakened" identity, the student came again to see the roshi, who was rude and dismissive. Hurt and confused, the student asked what he had done to offend the master. The roshi turned to him and asked, "Who do you think you are to claim satori?" The wisdom of all sages is that a person who clings to nothing will never gain or lose anything.

Awakening is at the heart of all spiritual traditions. Songs of liberation are celebrated by mystics and sages in all times and places. Each melody is a unique variation, an individual song honoring the theme of freedom. The poetry and music of awakening encourage us to cultivate the rich potential of solitude and listening, of engagement and life. They are songs of peace, joy, wisdom, compassion, and serenity. The words of freedom we listen to touch us deeply, awakening within our hearts an intuitive sense of possibility. We not only long to follow in the footsteps of the ancient sages, but also to discover the freedom they celebrate. An awakened teacher remarks, "Sitting quietly, doing nothing, spring comes and the grass grows by itself."

At times, awakening is described as "blowing out the fire," "extinguishing thirst," "cooling the flames," or "emerging from a dream." The awakened mind is timeless, limitless, vast, free, all encompassing, and joyful. Over the centuries seekers and aspirants have gone to the stillness of deserts and caves, into monasteries and temples seeking a profound inner realization of freedom. In the 1960s and 1970s hordes of young people traveled to Asia and sat at the feet of masters, continuing the tradition of pilgrimage. Some of us believed that freedom awaited us the moment we crossed the border into India. Soon we discovered that awakening was not geographical and that wisdom had no nationality. Our capacity for creating new forms of illusion knew no boundaries.

Listening to the songs of liberation, we are tempted to think that awakening will be a result of heroic effort, will arrive in the form of a headline experience, grand revelation, or pivotal breakthrough. We may bring to our search the expectancy of having a 'Bodhi tree' experience that will signal the end of all suffering. We envision a linear path of awakening, dependent upon the elimination of obstacles on our way to an experience of idealized Buddhahood. We think of freedom as a result, but liberation that is a *result* of anything continues to be a conditioned experience, subject to change and loss.

The Mystery of Awakening

There is a mystery to awakening. It is far away, yet offered to us in each moment of our lives. Awakening is as close as our own breath, yet it requires great effort to realize it. Through meditative disciplines there are a variety of profound mystical experiences it is possible for us to taste—experiences of stillness, emptiness, the dissolution of mind and body, vastness, and joy. Some of these are truly "breakthrough" experiences in that they shatter our illusions and beliefs and change our understanding of reality. They are not accidents; they follow in the wake of profound dedication, effort, investigation, and attention. Yet none of these could be said to be the direct cause of the moments of breakthrough. Through our sustained cultivation of dedication, effort, and investigation we learn to cultivate an inner environment that is receptive to profound wisdom. There is no practice or technique of awakening, but there are practices in which great simplicity is cultivated. There is a Christian saying: "For God to visit there must be nobody home."

The mystery of awakening is that it is not predictable, producible, or bound in time. Our expectations, hopes, images, and strivings only seem to get in the way of awakening. Ananda, a disciple of the Buddha, accompanied and served the Buddha throughout his life. The Buddha taught and, according to the stories, thousands were awakened by his words. It seemed that only Ananda was exempt from the contagion of enlightenment. There came a time when the first council of Arahants, or enlightened beings, was convened, and those who had undergone a profound inner transformation were invited to attend. As the time for the council meeting grew closer, Ananda practiced his meditation day and night, determined to find his own breakthrough and liberation. In the early hours before dawn, on the day of the meeting, Ananda, exhausted and despairing, finally admitted to himself that it was time to give up, accepting that he was never to be awakened. In the moment of his surrender, going to lie down upon his mat, the world stilled and there came to Ananda a transforming understanding of reality.

If we pursue awakening, it retreats from us. If we demand enlightenment, it hides. If we dismiss awakening, we dismiss ourselves. All that we can do is make ourselves enlightenment-prone. We learn to treasure the possibility of awakening in all moments and circumstances. We learn to simplify and cultivate the receptivity of heart that can be touched by profound understanding. We learn to listen deeply and discover stillness amid the movement in our world. The sage Teitiku taught:

> the morning glory blooms but a single hour,
> yet it differs not at heart,
> from the great pine that lives for a thousand years.

The Buddha was a mystic. The word Buddha translates as "awakened one". His life was dedicated to encouraging profound awakening and freedom. Conveying the essence of his teaching he said, "There is the unborn, uncreated, and unconditioned. Were there not the unborn, uncreated, and unconditioned, there would be no release for the born, created, and conditioned. Since there is the unborn, uncreated, and unconditioned, so there is release." He described the liberated person as the happiest person in the world, free from obsessions, worries, and troubles, not dwelling on the past or brooding over the future, but an awakened presence. Inner awakening enables a fullness of enjoyment and appreciation of life in its deepest sense without self-projection. Awakening is joyful, exultant, serene, and peaceful.

The Buddha was also *not* a mystic. Nowhere does he promise a freedom divorced from the grist of our everyday lives. Nowhere does he speak of a disembodied, transcendent experience or realm. The Buddha encourages us to remove the dust from our eyes. Awakening is here and now, in the stones of the rivers, the sunbeams on the grass, in this very body, mind, and life. Nowhere is there the encouragement to annihilate life, but simply to let go of our illusions. In being both a mystic and not a mystic, the Buddha ended the long schism between the sacred and the mundane, and the tension of being pulled in opposing directions. We are not invited to transcend the world but to dive deeply into it and find wisdom. We are asked to be in the world, but not of it—to cling to nothing, to reject nothing. Awakening invites our acknowledgement that we are social, sexual, spiritual embodied beings. Embracing our wholeness, we are alert to the doors of awakening offered to us throughout our life. We are Buddhas with amnesia, learning to remember ourselves.

Dedicated Moments of Stillness

There can be immense benefit is seeking places of solitude and stillness, removing ourselves for periods of time from the bustle of the world. If we bring our aversion to the world with us into these sacred spaces, we also bring the bustle. If we learn to enter into sacred spaces with the intention to be awake and listen fully, they deepen and enrich us. We learn powerful lessons of letting go, of stillness and sensitivity. We learn the lessons of freedom that are offered in the meandering thought, the fleeting sensation, in the heart of sorrow and joy. We learn to live in harmony with what is, to discover the spaces between thoughts and the stillness between sounds. We explore the profound stillness that embraces the gaps between the events and the events themselves.

We discover how vast and encompassing our hearts can be, and that wisdom has no end. The freedom of not resting upon anything, not being defined by anything, not wanting or missing anything, not being captive anywhere. Stillness and awareness are the nature of the mind unobstructed by grasping. Compassion is born of the understanding of emptiness. Within this world of arising and passing forms, of life in all its shapes and bodies, there is nothing separate from ourselves. In listening deeply to the world, understanding the causes of suffering and the way to its end, no other response is possible but compassion. Aware but still, we are awakened by the "10 thousand things."

Discovering these sacred spaces of stillness, we are encouraged to approach life in a sacred way. Great moments of illumination do not only belong to the recluses of this world, but are found in the hearts of ordinary people, extraordinary in their capacity to be awakened by their life. A couple raising and nurturing a profoundly disabled child, speak of it as a spiritual journey. The sleepless nights, the constant care, the surrender of personal freedom teaches them new depths of kindness, patience, and generosity. A young Tibetan nun thanks her torturer for awakening her to new depths of faith, compassion, and forgiveness. A teacher speaks of approaching her day as an opportunity to awaken just one child to new possibilities. A former athlete, debilitated by chronic fatigue, tells of the discovery of trust, humility, and kindness amid his helplessness. The essence of all spiritual teaching encourages us to turn toward our life and discover a freedom that leans upon nothing and embraces everything.

A philosopher once remarked, "When the facts change, I change my mind. What do you do, sir?" When our illusions are shattered by the intrusion of reality, we are asked to change, to enter unfamiliar territory and to let go. Teaching a retreat in Israel, I came out of the office one morning to find one of the resident dogs lying asleep, with a massive tumor growing on the top of his head. Stunned into silence by the horror of his condition, I could only look. It was a momentary silence, followed by an inner voice wondering at the apparent indifference of the residents who could let the dog suffer in this way. That voice gave way to one of compassion that accompanied me through the morning. With all my heart I offered loving kindness to the dog, "May you be free from suffering. May you be peaceful." At lunch, visiting the office again, I found the dog sitting up with his tumor on the ground beside him. It was a desert stone, identical in color to the fur of the dog. It was a moment of awakening. To understand what is real and true each moment we are always invited to probe beneath appearances.

The End of Sorrow

The ancient teachers encourage us to contemplate this fleeting world as: "A star at dawn, a bubble in the stream, a flash of lightning in a summer cloud, a flickering lamp, a phantom, a dream." It is not an invitation to dismiss, devalue, reject, or escape from this life, body, heart, and mind. Rather it encourages us to discover the vast, spacious, encompassing awareness of stillness and freedom. Rising from the Bodhi tree, the Buddha said, "I have done what needs to be done, seen what needs to be seen. This is liberation." Throughout his life he pointed the way to awakening in the profound simplicity of the Four Noble Truths. There is anguish and unsatisfactoriness in this life, there is the cause of sorrow, there is the cessation of sorrow in awakening, and there is a path to the end of sorrow.

Sorrow and unsatisfactoriness are evident; we do not have to search far. The cause the Buddha spoke of lies in the alienation of the truth manifested in "unquenchable thirst." The end of sorrow is in awakening to what is authentic and true—understanding the fleeting, transparent nature of all things, we hold nothing to be absolute, fixed, or solid. Releasing ourselves from clinging, illusion, and dependency, we are released from fear, agitation, and obsession. We discover what it means to be awake in all moments of our life. The path to the end of sorrow is not found outside our life in a philosophy or system, but in the very grist of it. We learn the art of understanding the simple truths in each moment, discovering what it means to be wise in our thought, speech, action, and livelihood. We learn to cultivate wisdom in our effort, mindfulness, and the way in which we attend to each moment of our life. Bringing heartfelt attention to each moment, we discover where we choose sorrow or limitation and where we choose freedom.

We always stand on the precipice of awakening. Each moment we listen deeply to life we cultivate the path of awakening. There are three questions we learn to bring to all the moments in our lives: "What to I need to cultivate in this moment to be truly awake? What do I need to let go of in this moment to be free? What do I need to learn from this moment to find profound peace?" Treasuring these questions we learn the lessons of freedom that life offers to us; they hold the power to return us to ourselves and to the heart of each moment. Awakening is not a destination but a way of seeing and of being.

In the silence of Zen sessions, students can be stunned to hear the roshi bellow the command, "Die on the cushion." Clearly it is not a command to keel over and expire, but to wake up from a dream. Awakening does not demand that we relinquish the world. Freedom invites us to relinquish our illusions, to open our eyes and hearts and discover the freedom available in each moment.

GUIDED MEDITATION

To discover what it means to be awake we need to find the honesty to acknowledge where we are lost in a dream. It may be the illusions we hold about ourselves or another person, the illusion of separation, or the opinions, conclusions, and beliefs we treasure. Our illusions are the places in our hearts and life where we feel most entranced or imprisoned. Do we find ourselves pursuing certainty and a life of guarantees? What do we avoid out of fear or aversion?

The most direct way to transformation is to turn a compassionate, warm attention to what we fear the most or cling to with the greatest tenacity. Where are our personal palaces of illusion? What is asked of us to be free? What do we need to cultivate, to let go of, or to learn, to find freedom in this moment?

beginner's mind

The real voyage of discovery lies not in finding new landscapes,

but in having new eyes.

MARCEL PROUST

A YOUNG woman returning from work was involved in a car accident that left her with severe head injuries. After several days in a coma, she awoke in hospital only to discover that she didn't know who she was. Not only had she forgotten herself but also everything and everyone in her life. Her initial panic was eased by the doctors' reassurance that her memory was likely to return. As the days passed in the hospital, she was much comforted by the visits from many kind people who spent time with her, who seemed to know who she was. There was one elderly man who spent hours by her bedside, sometimes reading to her, sometimes telling her stories of her life, and often just sitting quietly with her. In the comfort offered by his undemanding presence, she could share the anxieties and fears so alive in her heart.

Her memory began to return, vague fragments and images triggering greater and greater detail, until her life and story were once again accessible to her. The recovery of her memory was not only a recovery of herself but also of everyone else in her life. The kind, undemanding man, she had been so reassured by, was her father, whom she shared a troubled history with. To their amazement they discovered that her recovery enabled them to pick up their arguments at the very point they had left them before her accident. Soon they found themselves fighting familiar battles and all the old stories were recycled. The peaceful, intimate moments they had shared during her crisis became distant memories, lost in the intensity of their frustration, impatience, and struggle with each other. Once in a while they would look at each other and remember those blessed moments when no history stood between them.

Tragedy and amnesia are not recommended ways to cultivate a beginner's mind. Yet the beginner's mind is a pivotal key to unlocking the peace of simplicity. It is the simple clarity of the beginner's mind that enables us to enter each moment, relationship, and encounter free of prejudice and history. The cultivation of the beginner's mind is what frees us to greet every moment in our life with an openhearted welcome, to see ourselves, other people, and all of life anew; to be able to make new beginnings.

We collect, store, and accumulate so much weight in this life. The thousands of thoughts, ideas, and plans we have are imprinted on our minds. We have engaged in countless conversations and have replayed many of them over and over again. We have moved from one experience to another, one encounter to another, and we think about them all. Information and knowledge has been gathered, digested, and stored, and we carry all of this with us. This input forms our story, the story we have about people, ourselves, and the world. Experiencing the chaos and turbulence of the saturated mind and heart, forgetfulness may look like a blessing. Yet our innate capacity to receive the world, a source both of complexity and of compassion, will always be with us.

Freedom Within Our Stories

Muriel Rukeyser wrote, "The Universe is made of stories, not atoms." A spiritual path is not an endeavor to divest ourselves of all our stories, but to learn the wisdom within them. Our story, with all its complexity, busyness, repetitiveness, joy, and sorrow, is the very place that we learn to cultivate a beginner's mind. Within our life story is held the essence of all stories; our story is a gate to understanding and freedom. Heroic efforts are made to erase and subdue the stories that pass through our minds. They are seen as obstacles and barriers, and are blamed for our confusion. There is an old Jewish saying, "If I was to be someone else, who would be me?" It is not our stories that are the problem; it is being lost in them that causes the complexity and struggle. Mistaking our stories for absolute truth is the source of alienation. By learning to find simplicity and calmness within our stories, they teach us authenticity, creativity, and compassion.

The information, learning, and experience held within our stories are what enable us to live and be skillful in this world. Imagine if we had to relearn how to drive every time we got in a car or had to reread the computer manual every time we sat at our desk. Apart from practical wisdom, most of our deepest life wisdom is found through our stories. All that we have ever learned about joy and sorrow, peace and conflict, intimacy and alienation, we have learned from our story and the interface between our personal story and the story of life. From the times we have stumbled and the mistakes we have made, we have learned how to return to balance. We have learned from our experiences of pain how to heal ourselves and our relationships. We have learned from our experiences of being adrift and confused to question what it is we most value and treasure in this life. These lessons are learned for ourselves, through our stories, and they teach us about pathways of simplicity, wisdom, and compassion. No prescription, formula, or strategy can be a substitute for the learning that takes place in our own hearts.

Being wise, open, and receptive in our story we learn the lessons of freedom. Lost in our story we appreciate the power it holds to deny and subdue the beginner's mind. Our story carries within it not only the lessons of peace and freedom, but also the fears, insecurities, judgments, opinions, and self-consciousness that can dramatically distort our capacity for

simplicity and receptivity. All of these are born of past experiences and encounters that are still carried with us, moment by
moment, into each new encounter, experience, and connection.

The Vocabulary of Seeing Anew

The beginner's mind has a simple vocabulary founded upon
questioning and the willingness to learn. There are Zen meditative traditions that rest upon bringing one simple question
into each moment: "What is this?" Whatever arises in our
hearts, minds, and bodies is greeted with a probing investigation. What is this thought, this body, this experience, this
feeling, this interaction, this moment? It is a question intended
to dissolve all assumptions, images, opinions, and familiarity.
It is a question that brings a welcoming presence into each
moment; a question that perceives neither obstacles nor
enemies; a question that appreciates the rich seam of learning
offered in every encounter and moment. It is an "every
moment" practice, in which our capacity to listen and attend
unconditionally is treasured as the means of transformation.

The expert's mind has a different vocabulary, expressing a
devotion to "knowing" deeper than the devotion to freedom.
The expert's mind is the mind entangled with its history,
accumulated opinions and judgments, and past experience. The
most frequently occurring word in the mind of the expert is
"again." What a long story the word "again" can carry. We can
sense the shutters of our heart closing as we whisper to ourselves, "This thought, this feeling, this pain, this person again."

The intrusion of the past with all its comparisons, weariness, aversion, or boredom has the power to create a powerful disconnection in that moment. The word "again" carries with it the voice of knowing, fixing, and dismissing, and with its appearance we say farewell to mystery, to wonder, to openness, and to learning. Whenever we are not touched deeply by the moment we say farewell to the beginner's mind. An ancient teacher reminds us, "There is great enlightenment where there is great wonder."

A friend told me of her experience working with the elderly in a nursing home specializing in the care of those with Alzheimer's disease. Much of her work was listening. Day after day the same stories were recounted to her by the residents. Some of the stories were retold in a perpetual loop of repetition without variation. At first she said she learned to "tune out," smiling and nodding, yet elsewhere in her mind. Gradually a change took place as she sensed the deep sincerity and need for connection held within each conversation. She began to notice that her charges told their story as if they had never told it before. Her task, she realized, was to bring exactly the same attitude to her listening. To listen as if this was the first time she had heard this story and her first encounter with this person. With that change of heart she found she brought new levels of respect and appreciation into each contact. All she had to do was to put aside the word "again," so filled with her own story. It is the beginner's mind that enables each of us to make new beginnings in our life.

In a spiritual path we learn to open the doors, closed by the word "again." We sense how it carries with it a world of

impatience, frustration, and weariness. The subtext of "again"
is the equally weighted word "no." We want to rid ourselves
of this repetitive person, make ourselves into someone else,
and change our world in that moment. We want to have new
thoughts, encounters, experiences, and feelings, so that we can
be happy, peaceful, mindful, and free. We learn to remember
that the happiness, peace, and freedom we seek relies upon us
seeing each moment through new eyes. A meditation teacher
listened to his student complain of the utter boredom of
observing his breath in meditation, hour after hour, hinting
that he was ready for a more exciting practice. The teacher
roared with laughter and responded, "Bored? If you're bored
with this go back and do it for another hundred hours. If
you're still bored, do it for a thousand hours. Still bored,
observe your breath until you learn to be present in each
breath as if it was your last."

There are times when the parade of our judgments, images,
and stories arises habitually, following well-worn grooves in
our mind. There are times when we carefully hoard them,
repeat them, and rely upon them, as if they protect us from
harm. They appear to create a world of familiarity, security,
and safety. Believing that we know the person before us, the
event we're experiencing, and the day we enter into, we believe
that this familiarity provides us with the strategies and
responses that will safeguard us from the unknown.

A bear, raised in captivity, was rescued from the circus and
taken sedated to the wilderness. Waking in the morning, hungry
and fearful, it began performing tricks, turning somersaults,

dancing, and juggling pinecones. A group of curious bears watched in amazement, until finally one asked what was going on. The fearful bear could only answer, "If I do this for long enough someone will feed me and care for me." We rely heavily upon strategies to protect us from harm and fear, but instead they may bind us to a painful or fearful past. Our images, judgments, and assumptions protect us from "not knowing"—an experience we see as fearful.

How much of the knowledge, information, and strategies of our story serve us well? In our life story we experience hurt, pain, fear, and rejection, at times caused by others, at others self-inflicted. Understanding what causes sorrow, pain, and devastation translates into discriminating wisdom, and we do not knowingly expose ourselves to these conditions. We are all asked to make wise choices in our lives—choices rooted in understanding rather than fear.

The Buddha used the analogy of a raft. Walking beside a great river, the bank we are standing on is dangerous and frightening and the other bank is safe. We collect branches and foliage to build a raft to transport us to the other shore. Having made the journey safely, supposing we picked up the raft and carried it on our head wherever we went. Would we be using the raft wisely? The obvious answer is "No." A reasonable person would know how useful the raft has been, but wisdom would be to leave the raft behind and walk on unencumbered.

Still Learning

We can all learn the wisdom held within our stories, knowing when they are needed to take us into the next moment of our life and when it is wise to leave them behind. We ask ourselves what it is we may need to leave behind if we are to enter into this moment, this encounter, or this relationship with receptivity, openheartedness, and a beginner's mind. Our story is our raft; we learn, we understand, and then we let go. We learn to leave behind the judgments and assumptions, and the exhilarating, wonderful moments of enlightenment. We learn how to make new beginnings in each moment of our life. Michaelangelo said it succinctly: "I am still learning."

What difference would it make if our relationships with others and ourselves rested upon this attitude of "still learning?" How would we approach our worst enemy, our fiercest inner demon, washing the dishes, or the most deeply ingrained habit in our life, if we could bring to them the openness to say, "I am still learning?" We begin to sense the way that the intrusion of the expert's mind often signals a departure of attention, a quality of disconnection in which we flee from where we are. By assuming there is no more to learn, we exile ourselves from the seam of richness and sensitivity offered by the everyday encounters of life.

A Christian mystic reminded us, "Every concept grasped by the mind becomes an obstacle in the quest to those who search." Concepts will continue to appear as long as our mind functions. Through our concepts we describe the world, articulate insights, remember, and plan. In the mind of wonder, concepts are not an end, but a beginning. As concepts arise in our mind, we can consent to their conclusions, parade all of our familiar associations and memories that confirm our judgments, and then withdraw our attention. We can also let them be just whispers passing through our mind, probe beneath them, and refuse to equate them with reality. We can learn to bring into each encounter a profound willingness to be touched, informed, taught, and changed. We cultivate eyes of innocence, the wonder of a child, and a heart that is deepened by the ordinary moments of our life.

The security that our judgments, images, and concepts appear to offer is that they convince us that there is no need to change our inner world of opinions, reactions, and conclusions. If we are fully convinced that someone is irritating, frustrating, and annoying, we feel fully justified in our own irritation, annoyance, and frustration. In the security of that justification we may feel no need to cultivate deeper levels of patience, acceptance, and kindness in our own heart. The "irritant" is judged, banished, and frozen through our concepts, and we do not feel called upon to cultivate a new beginning in our relationship with them. If I know something to be boring, worthless, or mundane, I may feel no need to explore what difference wholehearted attention would make. If I convince myself that I am wounded, powerless, or inadequate, and accept this inner description, it is unlikely that I will feel a powerful yearning for freedom or wholeness.

Learning to dive beneath our concepts, conclusions, and assumptions, we learn to live with respect, reverence, and a divine curiosity. We find the wisdom to acknowledge that "knowing" is not always the same as wisdom and we open the doors of our heart to new beginnings in each moment. Cultivating the kindness and compassion of total attention, moments of wonder and mystery find their way into our life. When nothing and no one is confined or imprisoned in any image, there emerges an acceptance and vastness of heart that embraces all things. The great poet, Kabir, wrote:

The blue sky stretches out, farther and farther,
The daily sense of failure recedes,
The damage I have done to myself fades,
A million suns come forth with light,
When I sit firmly in that world.

The beginner's mind holds within it a generosity of heart that liberates us from the shackles of the self-images and conclusions that bind us endlessly to the wheels of the past. We are free to begin again, to understand ourselves deeply, and to be present. The beginner's mind is a key not only to personal freedom—it also liberates the people in our life, the world, and each moment from the chains of our assumptions, "knowledge," and ancient stories. The historical feuds, anger, and separation sustained by the fearful guarding of our judgments, begin to crumble before the generosity of the beginner's mind. The beginner's mind is the forgiving mind, listening, sensitive, and receptive.

New Beginnings

The cultivation of the beginner's mind asks for a powerful attention. New beginnings are always possible and in each new beginning we catch a glimpse of freedom. Those new beginnings are not a denial of history, nor of the wisdom gleaned; they are a release from history and are in themselves moments of joy. The long history of our stories, the ancient wounds we carry inwardly, the historical disputes we have with another person, are altered and transformed by our deep willingness to see anew, to begin anew.

An Israeli settler and an Israeli Arab spoke of the moment they found themselves trapped in an alley, caught in the crossfire between warring factions. As the bullets flew overhead they looked at each other and saw their own terror, anger, and panic reflected in each other's eyes. Later, both spoke of that moment when they hung between the extremes of wanting to harm the other and asking for each other's help. The healing and possibilities of new beginnings rest upon our capacity to choose freedom over suffering. True attention is vital. When engaged it holds within it the willingness to be changed by life, by our encounters with others and with each ordinary moment.

Cultivating the beginner's mind involves a leap of faith, a willingness to dive deeply into "not knowing." The alternative is to be chained to a past we know too well and to perpetuate history in each moment of our lives. In each new beginning we learn the art of letting things be. The concepts, images, assumptions, conclusions, and judgments; we let them be. They are received, listened to, and embraced in a vastness of heart that invests no absolute truth in them. It is a great challenge, undertaken only one moment at a time. Who is more free, the person who travels through their life carrying their raft upon their head, or the person who can lay it down and walk on unencumbered? The lessons of joy and sorrow, contraction and vastness, imprisonment and freedom are learned in each moment we are willing to begin anew and be changed by those lessons. They are simple and profound. To begin anew, to see anew, is to discover joy and freedom.

Make
www.thorsonselement.com
your online sanctuary

Get online information, inspiration
and guidance to help you on the path
to physical and spiritual well-being.
Drawing on the integrity and vision
of our authors and titles,
www.thorsonselement.com
is a great alternative to help create
space and peace in our lives.

www.thorsonselement.com

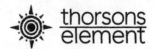

thorsons
element

CPSIA information can be obtained
at www.ICGtesting.com
Printed in the USA
LVHW010852020920
664557LV00001B/15

9 780007 323616